Asteroid Apophis
and
The Apocalypse

by
Njord Kane

Asteroid Apophis and the Apocalypse
by Njord Kane

© 2017 by Njord Kane. All rights reserved.

No part of this book may be reproduced in any written, electronic, recording, or photocopying form without written permission of the author, Njord Kane, or the publisher, Spangenhelm Publishing. You must not circulate this book in any format.

Published on: December 1, 2017 by Spangenhelm Publishing

Interior Design and Cover by: Njord Kane

ISBN-13: 978-1943066261

ISBN-10: 1943066264

1. Religion 2. Astronomy 3. Prophecy 4. Bible Prophecy

First Edition.

10 9 8 7 6 5 4 3 2 1

Table of Contents

Preface..i
Chapter 1...1
Chapter 2...25
Chapter 3...33
Chapter 4...45
Chapter 5...53
Chapter 6...59
Chapter 7...65
Chapter 8...71
Chapter 9...75
Chapter 10...81
Chapter 11...89
Chapter 12...99
Chapter 13...113
Chapter 14...125
Chapter 15...129
Sources..137

Preface

You may or may not be aware of this, but there's an asteroid headed towards us named, 'Apophis 99942'.

If you weren't aware, then here's your warning:

"Hey, NASA announced that there's an asteroid headed towards us".

Don't panic.

During the Christmas holiday of 2004, the international scientific community warned the public of an asteroid approaching expected to impact Easter Sunday 2036. Before news spread, the devastating Indian Ocean earthquake and tsunami occurred the following day.

The public immediately forgot about Asteroid 2004 MN4 as news of the tsunami dominated the media.

In 2004, a team of world renowned astronomers detected an asteroid hidden in the Sun's glare which had an orbital path heading directly towards Earth. The asteroid was named Apophis 99942 (Asteroid 2004 MN4) and is calculated to have a near-earth passover on April 13th, 2029, which will be clearly visible from the ground.

After it passes over 'scary close' in 2029, it will continue it's now altered orbit by gravitational attraction and return seven years later, impacting Earth on Easter Sunday, April 13, 2036 with 750 megatons of kinetic energy estimated to initially wipe out more than 10 million people.

Undeniably, this will cause an apocalypse.

All of this information you can check and verify yourself. In fact, I implore you to do so.

Find out hard-core verifiable facts of what scientists (astrophysicists, NASA, etc..) know about this asteroid and what they say is going to happen. What information do they have about its size and when it is going to impact us.

From a Christian perspective, the math along with historical records of this apocalyptic event match according to what we know of biblical prophecy and of what Christ tried to explain to us during His Ministry.

It's just something you can't ignore. Weight out the information yourself.

Chapter 1

Like a thief in the night

The Discovery of the Asteroid

If you read the preface then you're already aware that there's a giant rock hurling towards us named Apophis 99942.

If you didn't read it then, *'hey,.. there's a giant rock hurling towards us named Apophis 99942'*.

What is Apophis 99942?

Apophis 99942, also known as Asteroid 2004 MN4, is a near-Earth asteroid that was discovered in 2004 which has an orbit path calculated by NASA to collide with the planet Earth in the very near future.

Initial observations of the approaching asteroid indicated a probability of up to 2.7% that it would **hit Earth on April 13, 2029.**

Ironically, this happens to fall on Friday the 13th.

However, later calculations and measurements have reduced this risk down to being a historically close approach of this asteroid near Earth on April 13, 2029.

It will, unfortunately, return seven years later on April 13, 2036 and impact Earth.

This time in 2036, April 13th will fall on a Sunday, Easter Sunday.

The Asteroid was discovered just after 9 p.m. on June 18, 2004 by astronomer David J. Tholen at the Kitt Peak National Observatory with the help of Roy Tucker and Fabrizio Bernardi.

Three well known and highly respected astronomers using some of the world's most sophisticated astronomical equipment available.

The observatory is located on Kitt Peak of the Quinlan Mountains in the Arizona-Sonoran Desert on the Tohono O'odham Nation.

This is about 55 miles west by southwest of Tucson, Arizona.

Aerial View of Kitt Peak National Observatory

The Kitt Peak Observatory is administered by the National Optical Astronomy Observatory (NOAO). The secluded Observatory is equipped with 24 optical and two radio telescopes. This Observatory's collection is the largest and most diverse gathering of astronomical instruments in the world.

As the day faded into darkness over Kitt Peak National Observatory in Arizona secuded mountains, David Tholen was scanning for asteroids in an astronomical blind spot. This 'blind spot' is right inside Earth's orbit where the sun's glare can overwhelm telescopes.

Telescopes are light gathering devices which rely heavily on light and darkness contrasts to see faint and small objects in space. When the brilliant light from the Sun comes in, much of the light's contrast disappears and even large bright objects become very difficult to see.

You can see the difference in "light pollution" from the image on the left and the same section of sky on the right. The light contrast lessens and fewer celestial objects can be seen.

This is the same problem with viewing objects inside of Earth's orbit because of the Sun's light.

Because of this 'light pollution' astronomers seek out secluded regions where there is minimal light pollution. To view anything always illuminated by the Sun from Earth's vantage point, you need a very secluded area and exceptional equipment.

This what David Tholen was doing at the Kitt Peak National Observatory using some of the most sophisticated equipment on the planet. in a remote location free of light pollution to scan a very difficult to see region in space.

David James Tholen is an astronomer at the Institute for Astronomy at the University of Hawaii. Dr. Tholen holds a PhD from the University of Arizona and specializes in planetary and Solar System astronomy. He is a discoverer of minor planets and known for the *'Tholen spectral classification scheme'* used on asteroids.

The first sign of the threat was no more than a speck on a star-streaked telescope image. Dr. Tholen wasn't even sure he found anything significant. He knew that objects lurking there could sometimes veer toward Earth, drawn in by gravitational attraction.

There was an object hiding in the astronomical 'blind spot' of the Sun's glare and sneaking up into Earth's orbit unseen like a *"thief in the night"*.

Even more so, it was approaching in a manner where gravitational attraction would pull it the rest of the way into Earth's orbit, eventually colliding.

Here's a brief explanation of 'gravitational attraction'.

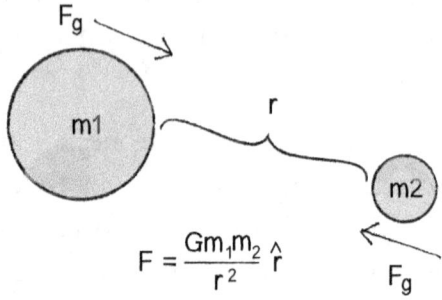

Gravitational Attraction is the force of attraction between all masses in the universe; especially the attraction of the earth's mass for bodies near its surface. In sum, objects with mass, such as planets and other large objects have their own gravity and that gravity is attracted to other masses. They draw and pull towards each other with the larger object pulling the smaller object towards it.

Spotting the object, Dr. Tholen enlisted the help of colleagues Roy Tucker and Fabrizio Bernardi.

Roy A. Tucker is a well known astronomer and prolific discoverer of minor planets who is credited by the Minor Planet Center with the discovery of 702 numbered minor planets between 1996 and 2010.

He has also discovered two comets:

328P/LONEOS–Tucker and *C/2004 Q1*,
a Jupiter-family and near-parabolic comet.

Fabrizio Bernardi is an astronomer and discoverer of minor planets and comets. He is a member of the International Astronomical Union (IAU) and credited by the Minor Planet Center with the discovery of seven numbered minor planets during 2002–2005. This includes *(280244) 2002 WP11*, another near-Earth object a member of the Amor group of asteroids and *(413666) 2005 VJ119*, a trans-Neptunian object.

In 2002, Fabrizio Bernardi discovered the outer main-belt asteroid *65001 Teodorescu* and named it after his wife, astronomer Ana Teodorescu. He also discovered *268P/Bernardi*, a Jupiter family comet.

These were some if the World's leading experts in obscure objects in our solar system.

They stared at the three images of the same section of sky cycle on the monitor's screen. The images which had been taken just a few minutes apart revealed the object's movement in the tail of our orbit.

"Here's your guy," said Tucker, pointing at a clump of white pixels that moved frame to frame across the images taken through the Observatory's telescope.

Flip through the next three pages to see the three images of Apophis and view it's movement via "flip-book animation".

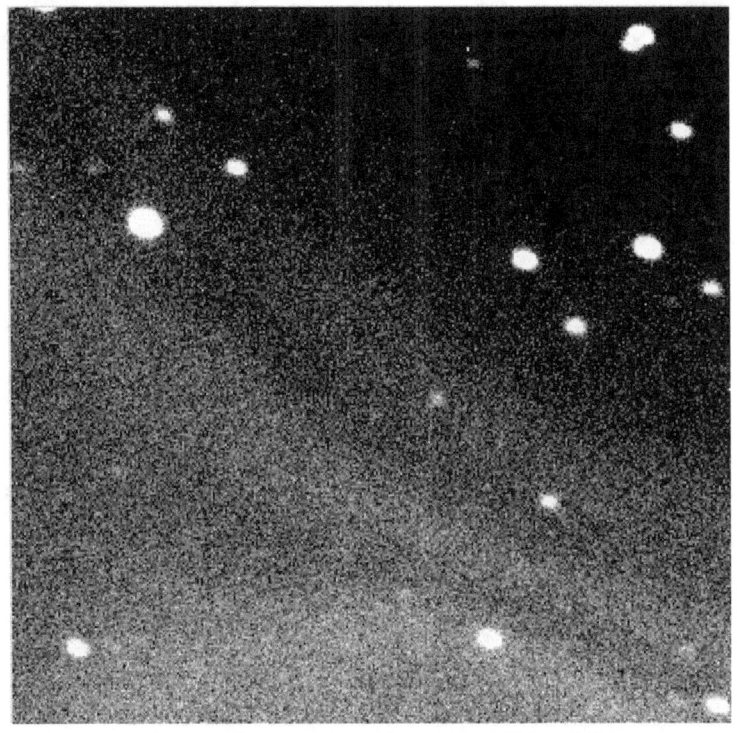

Image 1: Planetoid 99942 Apophis (2004 MN4) CCD images taken at Sormano on December 30, 2004.

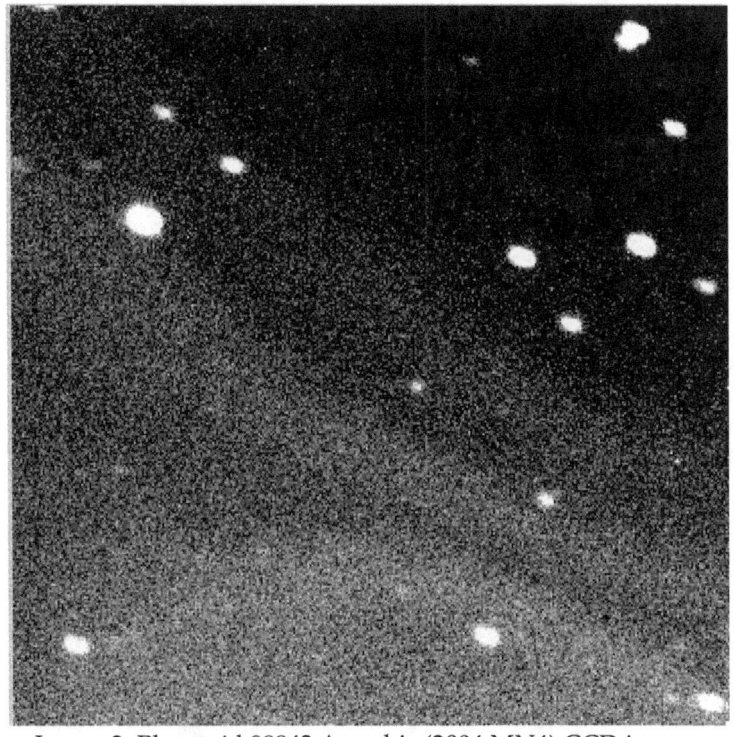
Image 2: Planetoid 99942 Apophis (2004 MN4) CCD images taken at Sormano on December 30, 2004.

Image 3: Planetoid 99942 Apophis (2004 MN4) CCD images taken at Sormano on December 30, 2004.

Dr. Tholen reported the sighting to the International Astronomical Union's Minor Planet Center, a clearinghouse for data on asteroids and comets.

When the object was first discovered on June 19, 2004 by these three prestigious astronomers, it was initially given the reference designation as:

Asteroid 2004 MN4

They were hoping to take another look at the object, now known as **2004 MN4**, later that week. Unfortunately, they were rained out and then the asteroid disappeared from view.

After Asteroid 2004 MN4 was rediscovered by G.J. Garradd at Siding Springs, Australia in December 2004, it was not only confirmed but also recognized as a potentially hazardous asteroid with a significant **Earth impact probability in April 2029**.

Later in December, astronomers got a fix on Asteroid 2004 MN4 again and that's when they realized they had a serious problem. They had tracked the object's orbit and the results were not looking very good at all.

On December 21st, Winter Solstice 2004, it was calculated that Asteroid 2004 MN4 passed approximately 14,410,000 km from Earth *(the Moon is 384,400 km)*.

The asteroid, which is bigger than a sports arena, was tumbling menacingly closer to our planet every few years. As observations streamed into the Minor Planet Center, the asteroid was becoming increasingly sinister.

"The impact hazard kept getting higher and higher," said Dr. Tholen in an interview with National Geographic Magazine.

Three days later on Christmas Eve 2004, Paul Chodas, Steve Chesley and Don Yeomans at NASA's Near Earth Object Program office calculated a 1-in-60 chance that 2004 MN4 would collide with Earth.

Impact date: April 13, 2029.

By Christmas of 2004, models were now predicting 1-in-40 odds that Asteroid 2004 MN4 would smash into Earth on April 13, 2029.

"One colleague called it *(the Asteroid)* the 'Grinch that stole Christmas'," Dr. Tholen said.

They were becoming more and more alarmed.

They made a formal announcement through the international media and the public was informed.

Then on December 26, 2004, a major catastrophe struck: the Indian Ocean tsunami, which claimed hundreds of thousands of lives.

The public immediately forgot about Asteroid 2004 MN4 as news of the tsunami dominated the media.

In the meantime, astronomers dug out earlier images of the asteroid to gather as much information on the object as they could. The extra data enabled the scientists to calculate the asteroid's orbit and they discovered that it would actually pass safely by Earth in year 2029.

A close call. It wasn't going to impact after all and instead pass 'scary close' on April 13, 2029.

There was still more work to be done. Pre-discovery recovery observations from March 15, 2004 were identified on December 27 and an improved orbit solution was then computed.

Radar astrometry in January 2005 further refined the Asteroid 2004 MN4's orbit solution.

Additional observations also provided improved calculations which helped eliminate the possibility of the asteroid impacting Earth or the Moon in the year 2029.

The image below is as close as current data places Asteroid 2004 MN4 to passing Earth in the year 2019.

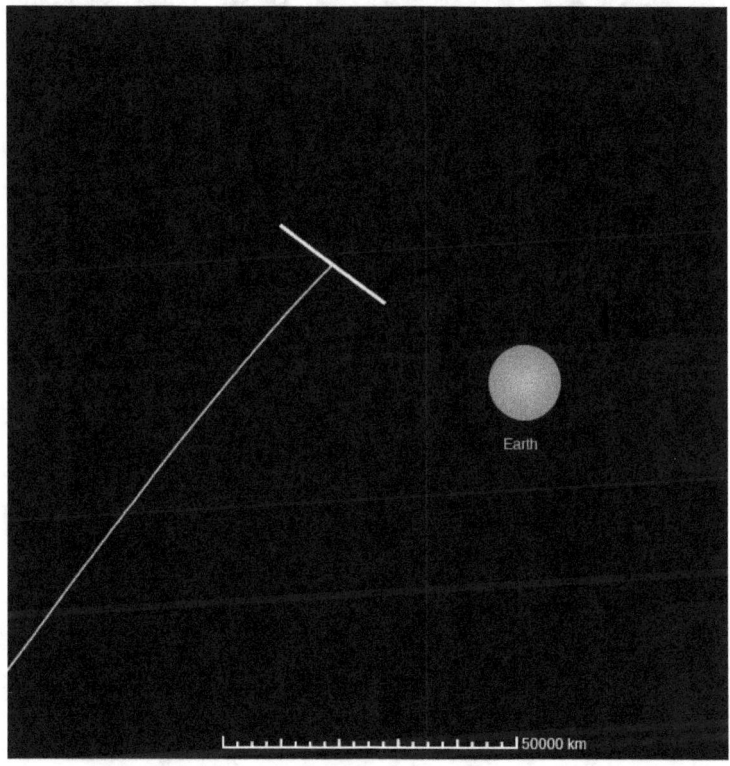

The white bar at the end of the trajectory line next to the representation of Earth indicates uncertainty in the range of positions (as known in February 2005).

When it comes past again in the year 2020, it will be closer and scientists will have a better gauge of the asteroid's orbit and size.

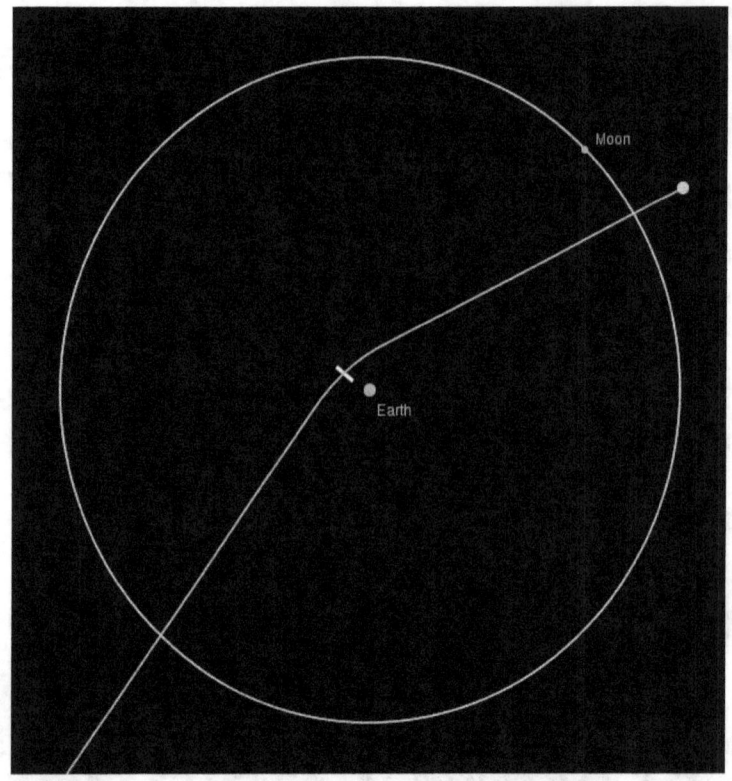

Close approach of Apophis on April 13, 2029
(as known in February 3, 2005).

Notice on the above image that Asteroid 2004 MN4's orbit will be changed while passing by the 'gravitational attraction' which was briefly explained on page 6.

When the asteroid passes in 2029, its orbit will be in orbital resonance with Earth. This will substantially increase the probability of a future impact in the year 2036.

Because of this change in the asteroid's orbit, scientists can no longer rule out the ever increasing chance that Apophis will strike with catastrophic effect on Easter Sunday, April 13, 2036.

Later on June 24, 2005, when the object's orbit was sufficiently well calculated, it received the permanent designation number of **99942**.

This permanent designation number made it eligible to be named and on July 19, 2005, Asteroid 2004 MN4 received the name "**Apophis**" by the discovery team.

In the August 18, 2005 copy of Astronomy Magazine, Bill Cooke explained the naming in his article, "Asteroid Apophis set for a makeover":

"Apophis is the Greek name of an enemy of the Ancient Egyptian sun-god Ra: Apep, the Uncreator, an evil serpent that dwells in the eternal darkness of the Duat and tries to swallow Ra during his nightly passage. Apep is held at bay by Set, the Ancient Egyptian god of storms and the desert.

David J. Tholen and Tucker—two of the co-discoverers of the asteroid—are reportedly fans of the TV series Stargate SG-1. One of the show's persistent villains is an alien named Apophis. He is one of the principal threats to the existence of civilization on Earth through the first few seasons, thus likely why the asteroid was named after him.

In the fictional world of the show, the alien's backstory was that he had lived on Earth during ancient times and had posed as a god, thereby giving rise to the myth of the Egyptian god of the same name."

According to the article, Asteroid 2004 MN4 was named 'Apophis' after the Egyptian god of death and uncreation. And this naming was based upon one of astronomer's favorite television shows?

Works for me and what an appropriate name when you think about it. If this asteroid hits us, it very well may be 'the uncreator'.

Here is a depiction of the 'uncreator' Egyptian god Apep (Apophis) as a serpent. His name is reconstructed by Egyptologists as *ʿA'pāpī, as it was written ꜥpp(y) and survived in later Coptic Greek as ⲁⲫⲱⲫ (Aphōph), later anglicized as 'Apophis'.

Ancient Egyptian art depicting Apep (Apophis from Coptic Greek: ⲁⲫⲱⲫ) being warded off by a deity.

The danger was averted, but there still remained the probability that during 2029 close encounter with Earth, asteroid Apophis would pass through a gravitational keyhole.

This 'keyhole' is a small region no more than about 600 miles wide that would pull in Apophis' orbit closer into Earth's. This 'gravitational' attraction' was calculated that it would set up a future impact exactly seven years later when it passed again.

This future impact date is:
Easter Sunder, April 13, 2036

In the year 2013, asteroid Apophis passed within 0.0966 AU (14,450,000 km; 8,980,000 mi) of Earth and allowed scientists to refine the trajectory for future calculations of close passes to come.

The next pass of the asteroid will be in the year 2020 and this time you'll be able to see it with a telescope (pending weather, light, etc.).

Chapter 2

How big is it?

The Asteroid's Size

Okay, so there's a giant rock named after an Egyptian god of death heading right for us.

That kills any plans I had for THAT day...

Asteroid Apophis 99942's size is estimated to be from about 330 meters (1,080 ft) to around 450 meters (1,480 ft).

Note: this estimated size will change in a few years as we get a closer look at it as it passes.

It's current size is estimated by the amount of light given off and by its approximate distance. So we don't have any accurate numbers at this current time. We do know that it's big.

Based upon the observed brightness, Apophis' diameter was initially estimated at 450 meters (1,480 ft). A more refined estimate based on spectroscopic observations at NASA's Infrared Telescope Facility in Hawaii by Binzel, Rivkin, Bus, and Tokunaga (2005) is 350 meters (1,150 ft).

NASA's Infrared Telescope Facility on Mauna Kea, Hawaii.

That's about 1/4 mile in size, give or take, or basically 3 1/2 to 5 footballs in diameter (wide, tall, and long).

Current size estimates of this giant rock range from about the length of a drag strip to being larger than the size of the Empire State Building.

Image Source: iluminaci.com

Bottom line, are we doomed?

This asteroid is not a planet killer *(at least I hope not - I live here too!)*, but it's still going to hurt.

The 'planet killer' that took out the dinosaurs less than 66 million years ago created the **Chicxulub impact crater** buried underneath the Yucatán Peninsula in Mexico. The Chicxulub impact crater was formed by a large asteroid or comet that was about 10 to 15 kilometers *(6 to 9 miles)* in diameter.

The impact that took out the dinosaurs was about 30 to 45 times bigger than the one *(Apophis 99942)* that's heading towards us now.

So, it's not the end of life on Earth.

But it may be the end to life as we know it.

Here is a visual of the Chicxulub impact that some scholars believe may have taken out the dinosaurs below:

Here is where it hit and the affect of the impact.

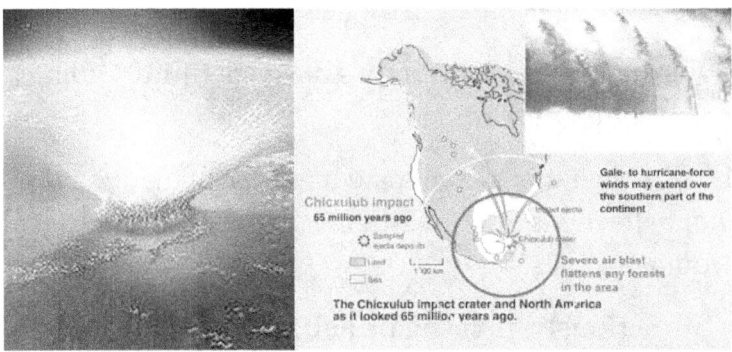

You can see where it hit the Yucatán Peninsula in the gulf of Mexico region.

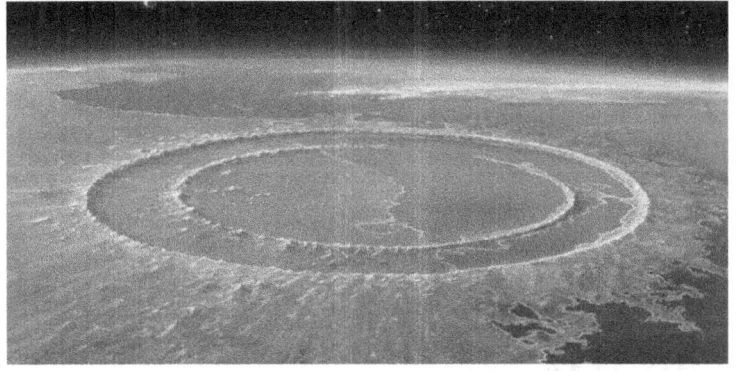

Artist's reconstruction of Chicxulub crater soon after impact, 66 million years ago. Source: sciencemag.org

That was the impact that scientists believe took out the dinosaurs.

The one coming at us now is not that big,.. but it's still going to hurt.

The one headed at us right now is still a 1/4 mile sized or larger rock hurling at us...

When it hits, somebody's day is definitely going to be completely ruined.

I realize this a lot to take in, so I ask that you do not believe me and investigate **Apophis 99942** yourself.

- Seriously, investigate and see for yourself.

I do hope you do, instead of simply taking my word. There is so much false information out there, check yourself.

When you do investigate this for yourself, you will notice they've downplayed it several times over recent years.

Well they must.

Can you imagine how everyone would be acting if they knew a rock the size of their neighborhood was coming at them?

It's probably best to go everyone goes about their business day to day in ignorance. There is nothing you can do about it anyways **and they are working on it.**

The next pass will be in the year 2020 (you'll be able to see with with a telescope then) and that will be when scientists will be able to gather accurate information about the asteroid's orbit.

Even still, they are not waiting until then to come up with solutions.

Chapter 3

What's being done about it?

Plans to Stop it

Now don't think just because it was discovered that its going to impact that the scientific community isn't planning on doing anything about it

In July 2005, former Apollo astronaut Russell Louis "Rusty" Schweickart, as chairman of the B612 Foundation, formally asked NASA to investigate the possibility that the asteroid's post-2029 orbit could be in orbital resonance with Earth, which would increase the probability of future impacts.

The B612 Foundation is a private nonprofit foundation headquartered in Menlo Park, California which is dedicated to planetary defense against asteroids and other near-Earth object (NEO) impacts.

Schweickart also asked NASA to investigate whether a transponder should be placed on the asteroid to enable more accurate tracking of how its orbit is affected by the Yarkovsky effect.

On January 31, 2011, astronomers took the first new images of Apophis in more than 3 years, confirming the effect on the asteroid's orbit.

China plans an exploration fly-by mission to Apophis 99942 after 2020 when the asteroid comes to within a distance of 30,000 kilometers of Earth.

30,000 km is about 18,600 miles or so and is but a hair's breadth in astronomical terms. The distance is within the orbit of the moon and even closer than some man-made satellites.

It will be the closest asteroid of its size in recorded history.

"The fly by mission to *Apophis (99942)* is part of an asteroid exploration mission planned after China's Mars mission in 2020 currently in development", according to Ji Jianghui, a researcher at the Purple Mountain Observatory of the Chinese Academy of Sciences and a member of the expert committee for scientific goal argumentation of deep space exploration in China.

"The whole mission will include exploration and a close study of three asteroids by sending a probe to fly side by side with Apophis for a period to conduct close observation.

It is also planned to land on *asteroid 1996 FG3* to conduct sampling analysis on the asteroid's surface.

The probe is also expected to conduct a fly-by of a third asteroid to be determined at a later time. The whole mission would last around six years," said Ji Jianghui.

The distance the asteroid Apophis will be passing Earth in the year 2020 is within the orbit of the Moon **and even closer than some man-made satellites**.

In fact, it may hit some satellites as it passes by.

This will be in 2020, so don't panic if your e-device and/or phone suddenly goes stupid and won't connect to services. Cable TV could go out too. Stock up on books, games, and hobbies just in case. Having a hefty DVD collection won't hurt either if you're not used to having the internet and cable TV all the time.

It's not the "End of the World" or Armageddon. No need to go hide in the caves with years worth of canned goods and toilet paper.

It just means your provider's satellite was just taken out by a giant rock hurling pass us in space.

Personally, I'm hoping we'll be able to see it from the ground with a telescope or binoculars.

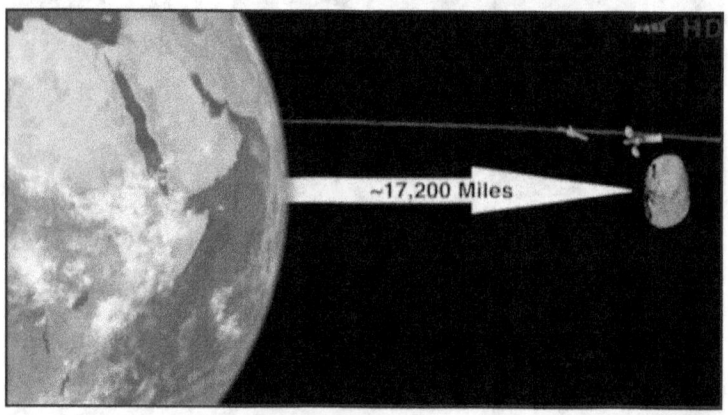

It also means your cell/cable/online services bills will probably go up soon because they have to replace the satellite now.

What will it look like and can we see it?

Yes, we will be able see it from our backyards with binoculars. Maybe smart phone cameras will be able to zoom in better by then as well.

News coverage will be widespread and will most likely grant the 'best view', but as I pointed out – their satellites may get hit and knocked out.

When it passes, it should be no different than it would be viewing a satellite or the International Space Station passing by.

It will be a point of light gliding across the sky, faster than many satellites, brighter than most stars.

Here is a picture of the International Space Station (ISS) passing by in the night sky, as an 'almost example':

International space station in the night sky.

I am sure it will be much more spectacular to watch than the ISS passing by *(sorry ISS, no offense)*. It may leave a tail behind due to its proximity to the planet, but I am by no means an expert.

The Chinese plan to fly up there and investigate it, so there's a show to watch when they go up as well.

It's an understatement to say that with the American Election, the Chinese Space Launch, and the passing of the Asteroid Apophis 99942, the years 2019 and 2020 will definitely be eventful.

Additionally, if the asteroid hits any satellites, there might be a cool light show worth watching.

And I'm not jinxing the Chinese, but if there's an error and they crash into it; there will be a pretty cool fireworks display that only the Chinese could deliver!

All joking aside, I truly hope nothing happens and the Chinese mission is highly successful.

China's asteroid exploration will help scientists better understand the basic features of the near-Earth objects, and seek effective measures to deal with the possibility of a collision.

I believe it will be an event worth planning to watch.

We'll have a more accurate day and time soon when the asteroid comes nearer to pass us in the year 2020.

What else are they doing about this giant rock hurling pass / at us?

The **Don Quijote mission** by the European Space Agency was used to gather data to study the effects of impacting an asteroid. There is no ruling out as of yet the feasibility or necessity of having to using missiles to break it up.

Simply launching a weapon at an asteroid is easier said then done. So is simply landing on it.

The **Rosetta space probe** was built by the European Space Agency for this mission and was launched on 2 March 2004. Along with Philae, its lander module, Rosetta performed a detailed study of the comet Churyumov–Gerasimenko *(comet 67P).*

On 6 August 2014, the spacecraft reached the comet and performed a series of maneuvers to eventually orbit the comet at distances of 30 to 10 kilometers (19 to 6 mi). On 12 November 2014, its lander module Philae performed the first successful landing on a comet, though its battery power ran out two days later.

Communications with Philae were briefly restored in June and July 2015, but due to diminishing solar power, Rosetta's communications module with the lander was turned off on 27 July 2016.

On 30 September 2016, the Rosetta spacecraft ended its mission by hard-landing on the comet in its Ma'at region.

There are also other proposed deflection Asteroid-impact avoidance strategies.

Studies by NASA, ESA, and various research groups in addition to the Planetary Society contest teams, have described a number of proposals for deflecting Apophis and similar objects, including gravitational tractor, kinetic impact, and nuclear bomb methods.

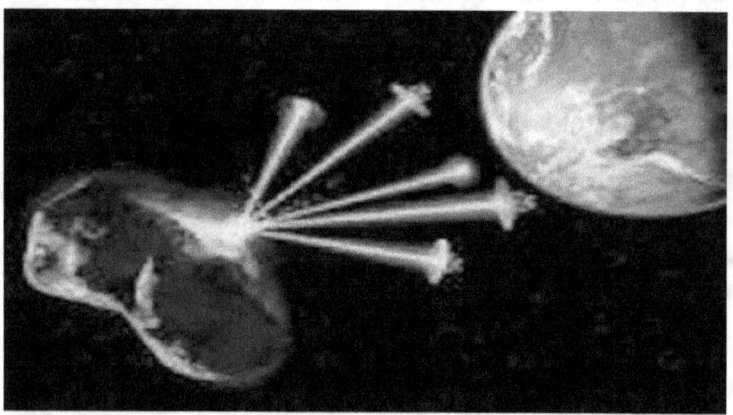

On December 30, 2009, Anatoly Perminov, the director of the Russian Federal Space Agency, said in an interview that Roscosmos (the science and space program of the Russian Federation) will also study designs for a possible deflection mission to Apophis.

On August 16, 2011, researchers at China's Tsinghua University proposed launching a mission to knock Apophis onto a safer course using an impactor spacecraft in a retrograde orbit.

This spacecraft will be steered and powered by a solar sail. Instead of moving the asteroid on its potential resonant return to Earth, Shengping Gong and his team believe the secret is shifting the asteroid away from entering the gravitational keyhole in the first place.

In sum, use solar sail spacecraft to gently pull the asteroid out of its orbit *BEFORE* it gets pulled into Earth's orbit and thus eliminating the danger.

On February 15, 2016, Sabit Saitgarayev, of the Makeyev Rocket Design Bureau, announced intentions to use Russian ICBMs to target relatively small near-Earth objects.

Although the report stated that likely targets would be between the 20 to 50 meters in size, it was also stated that Apophis 99942 would be an object subject to tests by the program.

As I mentioned, they're working on it.

There's not much we can do but relax and watch.

Study hard in school and help them come up with feasible solutions, perhaps?

Also worth mentioning, The Planetary Society, a California-based space advocacy group, organized a $50,000 (USD) competition in 2007 to design an unmanned space probe that would 'shadow' Apophis 99942 for almost a year. The probe would be taking measurements that would help governments decide whether to mount a deflection mission to alter its orbit.

The society received 37 entries from 20 countries on 6 continents. Although there were winners with feasible designs, none of the projects were launched into action.

As for now, they're still working on it.

Once it passes in **2020**, it won't be back for another **9 years**.

The next passing of Apophis 99942 near Earth will be on April 13, 2029.

When Apophis 99942 passes very near Earth on April 13, 2029, it just so happens that it will be on Friday the 13th. It is also the day before the New moon in April 2029. Most folks of the Jewish Faith know what that means – Passover *(sort of ironic)*.

This is the asteroid's passing which has scientists

concerned and why there are projects to find ways to deal with this object.

This time it when it passes, it will be much closer and it will be a much greater threat.

We won't need binoculars to see it when it passes us in April of 2029 .

It will look much like the meteor passing in 2004, but WAY BIGGER!

Photograph of meteor over Russia in 2004.

It will be VERY close, under our satellites (we will get better estimates in 2020 when it passes) and it will leave a grand show across the sky. The smaller meteors with it will burn up and split out as well for more fireworks in the sky.

Once it passes in **2029**, it won't be back for another **7 years**.

Chapter 4

Easter 2036

The Final Approach

The final approach of Apophis 99942 will happen on Easter Sunday, April 13, 2036.

This time scientists say it will hit us. When it passes us in 2029, the gravitational attraction will draw the asteroid's orbit into an impact path into our planet.

Asteroid Apophis 99942 will hit us in the year 2036 unless we've come up with a solution to destroy or divert it by then.

The B612 foundation produced a paper for the 2007 Planetary Defense Conference with a calculated path of risk for the projected 2036 impact.

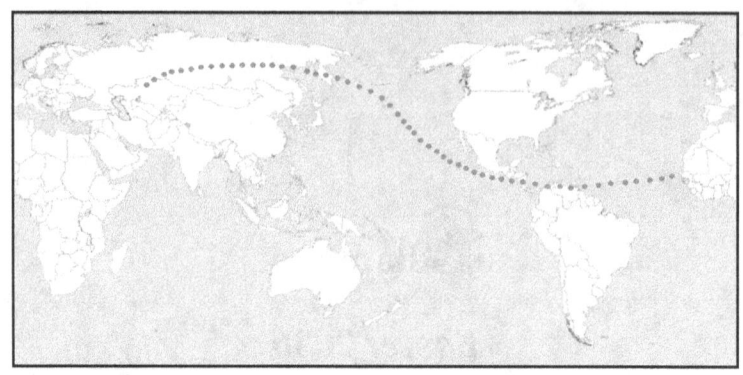

The B612 foundation produced a paper for the 2007 Planetary Defense Conference with a calculated path of risk for 2036.

So what kind of damage can we expect?

Using the computer simulation tool NEOSim, it was estimated that the impact of Apophis 99942 in countries such as Colombia and Venezuela, which were in the path of risk, could have more than **10 million casualties**.

The force of impact as estimated by the Sentry Risk Table (Earth Impact Risk Summary – NASA) estimates that Apophis 99942 would make atmospheric entry with **750 megatons of kinetic energy**.

In comparison, the meteor impact (air explosion) from the **Tunguska Event** in Russia on 30 June 1908 is estimated to be only in the **3–10 megaton** range. the object is thought to have disintegrated at an altitude of 5 to 10 km (3 to 6 mi) rather than hit the surface of the Earth.

The Tunguska event is the largest impact event on Earth in recorded history. Studies have yielded different estimates of it's size, on the order of 60 to 190 meters (200 to 620 feet), depending on whether the body was a comet or a denser asteroid.

The 15 megaton estimate represents an energy about 1,000 times greater than that of the atomic bomb dropped on Hiroshima, Japan — roughly equal to that of the United States' Castle Bravo (15.2 megaton) ground-based thermonuclear detonation on 1 March 1954.

Impact area of the Tunguska Event in Russia on 30 June 1908.

The 1883 volcano eruption of Krakatoa was the

equivalent of roughly 200 megatons.

The pressure wave generated by the volcanic explosion radiated out from Krakatoa at 1,086 km/h (675 mph) and was loud enough to be heard clearly 5,000 km (3,100 mi) away.

The pressure wave from the explosion was recorded on barometers all over the world. Several barometers recorded the wave seven times over the course of five days: four times with the wave traveling away from the volcano to its antipodal point, and three times traveling back to the volcano. Hence, the wave rounded the globe three and a half times. Ash was propelled to an estimated height of 80 km (50 mi).

That's only 1/3 of the estimated impact energy that is expected from Apophis 99942 in April 2036. The impact of Apophis 99942 will be equivalent to three Krakatoa eruptions.

That's huge, but it will not be as big enough to kill the entire planet.

The biggest hydrogen bomb ever exploded was the Tsar Bomba and it was around 57 megatons.

Apophis 99942 will be equivalent to 10-12 of these hydrogen bombs.

This will be an extremely large and deadly

impact, but it is NOT a planet killer. There will be global disasters and deaths at a biblical scale, but we WILL survive.

However, the **Chicxulub Impact** at the Yucatan Peninsula that is believed to have taken out the dinosaurs and forever changed life on planet Earth has been estimated to have released about as much energy as **100,000,000 megatons**.

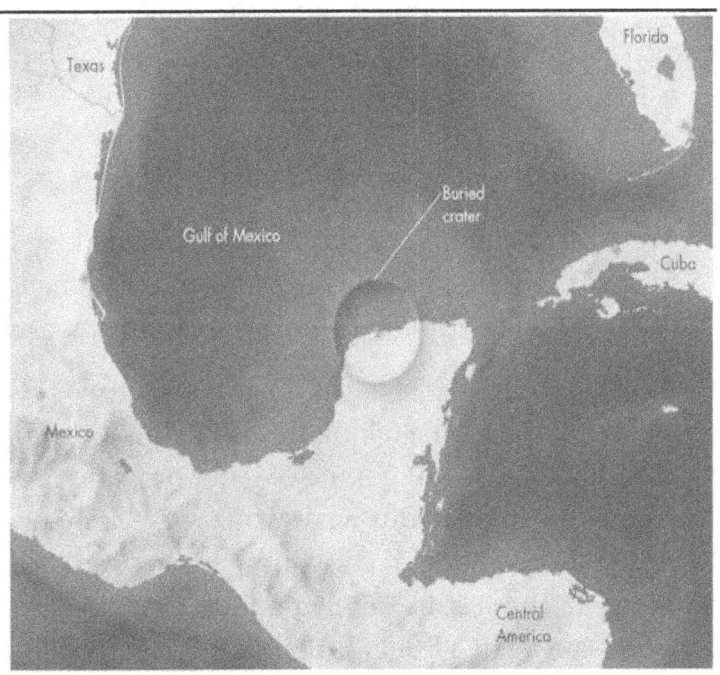

The Chicxulub Impact crater at the Yucatan Peninsula (Gulf of Mexico)

Is all life doomed?

49

No. Apophis 99942 is NOT a planet killer like the asteroid that hit when dinosaurs walked.

So they estimate a force 3 to 4 times larger than the Krakatoa Volcano eruption with an estimated casualty count of approximately 10 million people.

When it hits us on April 13, 2036, it is estimated to be a 750 Megaton "bomb" with an estimated human causality rate of 10 million.

BOOM.

The Apocalypse. *(pause for dramatic effect)*

Well, that definitely explains why they don't seem to care about what they're doing to the planet. They seem to be stripping its resources for profit and polluting it like there's no tomorrow.

I know I seem to be taking this rather lightly and it's not just because I'm getting old and probably won't make it to then. But what would panicking or worrying do besides make my life a misery until the day comes? There's absolutely nothing I can do about it, save plan a BBQ for that day. Find a good place to watch with lawn chairs and coolers.

They are working on it.

We have until 2036 to figure out how to stop or deflect it. **FUND YOUR SCHOOLS!**

Whether this is biblical or simple what we dream up in science fiction novels, this asteroid impact will not kill the planet, but its aftermath will cause an Armageddon.

If you're religious, I highly recommend that you *'get right with the Lord'*.

I know, a rather cliche' statement, but check out these next chapters and you may want to re-think things..

...or not, that's completely up to you.

Check out *(drumroll)* **The Prophecies** in the next chapters.

Chapter 5

The Prophecies

What was foretold

You know what, I try not to worry about things of which I have absolutely no control over. However that doesn't stop my curiosity.

I know all of this is all going to sound ludicrous, because I know it does to me. I really don't know what to make of it all and it's probably just a weird coincidence.

A perfect coincidence of both prophesied and told events that just happen to occur perfectly. I say "prophesied and told" because of the prophets that foretold of the events by dreams and visions are "prophesied events"; and "told events" are events that Jesus straight out told us were going to happen.

He told us what, why, when, and described it in detail.

It required faith until now (He even mentioned that too). Now you have science telling you it's coming.

I ran across this information while seeking answers to something else, specifically what is NASA was doing about the approaching near object, asteroid Apophis 99942.

I noticed when it was announced in the international news in 2004 and 2005. I noticed the contest for feasible solutions – even joked about it with friends. I noticed the international astrological and space communities all working together for answers.

But like everyone else, I got busy with life and side tracked. There was plenty of time and I figured they probably had a solution by now.

They do not.

The fact it was striking the year 2036 on Easter Day was what got my attention. I remembered reading somewhere that the year 36 AD was one of the dates historians and biblical scholars believed to be when Jesus was crucified. This was when I remembered the rest of the biblical dates and prophesied timelines.

Now mind you, I am not a religious guy and I definitely wasn't looking for anything religious in this asteroid. I was just curious as to what progress has been made on it thus far. But then I noticed a few things.

Anyways, here is what I realized:

- The discovery of the Asteroid was on the 2000th anniversary of Christ's celebrated birth on Christmas Eve 2004.

- The first near Fly-by affecting Earth noticeably with be on the 2000th anniversary of when Christ was baptized and entered his ministry. When Jesus became "Christ" and was filled with the Holt Spirit and began to deliver His message of Salvation.

- The impact date of 2036 will be on the 2000th anniversary of when Jesus rose from the dead after being crucified. On the third day he was risen, The Resurrection.

Ooooh, did I just get your attention? Allow me to break it down and explain so you can check your own bibles.

You're going to want to, trust me.

Matthew 25:13 (NIV) Therefore keep watch, because you do not know the day or the hour.

We are told that we will not know the day or the hour of His coming, but we are also told that we will know when it is near.

Matthew 24:33 (NIV) Even so, when you see all these things, you know that it is near, right at the door.

Signs were given to us for a reason.

Chapter 6

The announcement

Establishing when Jesus was born

Establishing when Jesus was born.

The exact date of Jesus' birth is not known to us.

We borrowed the holiday 'Christmas' from pagans to celebrate the birth of Christ as 'Christ's Mass'.

With that being said, we can still gander a pretty good 'guesstimate' of when He was born. There are two approaches which are generally used to 'guesstimate' the birth year of Jesus:

> 1. The accounts of His birth in the Gospels with reference to King Herod's reign,
> 2. By working backwards from His stated age of "about 30 years" of when he began

delivering His message of Salvation.

Christ's birth is not the year 0 or 1 AD of our current year count because our calendars have changed several times over the centuries since then.

The calendar most universally used today is the Gregorian Calendar introduced in October 1582 AD by Pope Gregory XIII.

The Julian Calendar was in place before that, which took effect January 45 BC. The Julian Calendar was a 365 days calendar with an extra day added every four years proposed by Julius Caesar to replace the Roman Calendar in place at Rome which was short a few days in the year.

A calendar was established that would be a combination between the old Roman months, the fixed length of the Egyptian calendar, and the 365 1/4 days of the Greek astronomy.

The first step of the reform was to realign the start of the calendar year (1 January) to the tropical year by making 46 BC (708 AUC) 445 days long, compensating for the intercalations which had been missed during Caesar's pontificate.

This year had already been extended from 355 to 378 days by the insertion of a regular intercalary month in February.

When Caesar decreed the reform, probably shortly after his return from the African campaign in late Quintilis (July), he added 67 more days by inserting two extraordinary intercalary months between November and December.

But that wasn't the only calendar in use during the period or region.

There was also the Alexandrian Calendar, the Asian Calendar and the Syro-Macedonian Calendar widely in use.

In sum, year 0 or 1 AD has moved around and changed a bit over the centuries as calendars were modified and adjusted over the years.

This isn't mentioning any lost records from events following Christ, such as the rebellions and the fall of Jerusalem and the Second Temple in the year 70 AD (we have an accurate date on that).

Using the aforementioned 'guesstimating' methods, most scholars believe the birth of Jesus to have been between the years 6 BC to 4 AD.

He was about "30-ish", so the year 4 AD is a good possibility, but in all honesty we simply do not know.

Some assume the birth of Jesus to be possibly the year 30 BC, counting backwards from year 0 (or 1 AD). This makes year 1 AD the first year "After

Death" from when He was crucified.

Sadly, we don't know for sure. Buy perhaps it answers as to why nothing happened in 1999/2000 during the whole Y2K scare.

Because of the asteroid's sighting announcement being on Christmas Eve 2004, I couldn't help "assuming" that was meant to mark his birth date having happened 2000 years ago.

When the sky announced His Arrival.

I found this to be very symbolic and quite frankly, that was enough for me to go on.

Scripture tells us that the skies were used to hail and announce His coming when He was born, I see absolutely no reason why this wouldn't be the case again.

Whether "Christmas" is His birthday or not, I am POSITIVE He knows we celebrate His birth on that day. Why wouldn't He announce His coming to the world on the 2000th anniversary of the day commonly celebrated as the day of His first arrival?

Especially when we're expecting His return to be after 2000 years (two days to the Lord) at the conclusion of Daniel's sixth week.

It really doesn't matter and isn't that critical, but given events, the year AD 4 sounds good to me.

The first celestial announcement of Jesus' coming (birth) was most probably in 4 AD.

The second celestial announcement of Jesus coming was 2000 years later in 2004 AD.

~

Jesus birth isn't as important as the following points in the next chapters which led me to believe the coming of this asteroid is strongly related to His return.

Chapter 7

The Gathering

Establishing Jesus' Ministry

There are three details of which have been used to estimate the year of when Jesus began His Ministry preaching the Gospel:

> 1. A mention of his age of "about 30 years" during "the fifteenth year" of the reign of Tiberius Caesar.
>
> 2. The date of the building of the Temple in Jerusalem.
>
> 3. The death of John the Baptist.

With this information, scholars estimate that Jesus began preaching and gathering followers at around AD 27-29. According to the three synoptic gospels Jesus continued preaching for at least one year, and according to John the Evangelist for three years.

John the Baptist Prepares the Way

> **Luke 3:1-2** (NIV) "**In the fifteenth year of the reign of Tiberius Caesar**—when Pontius Pilate was governor of Judea, Herod tetrarch of Galilee, his brother Philip tetrarch of Iturea and Traconitis, and Lysanias tetrarch of Abilene—²during the high-priesthood of Annas and Caiaphas, the word of God came to John son of Zechariah in the wilderness."

The reign of Reign Tiberius Caesar was from **18 September 14 AD to 16 March 37 AD** (22 years).

The 15th year of the reign of Tiberius Caesar was in 29 AD,

Luke places the ministry of John the Baptist to have began in 29 AD and the baptism of Jesus is generally considered as the start of His ministry (which was shortly after the start of the ministry of John the Baptist).

> **The Spirit came to man in 29 AD, ending the 4th week, and beginning the 5th week of Daniel.**

This is when the **Epiphany** occurred. It is when Jesus was recognized as being.... Jesus. It is celebrated on January 6th by the Church as being the most probably time he began his Ministry, but I disagree.

Say we go with the evidence the Church has and go with January 6th. After being baptized by John and having the Spirit descend upon him like a dove, he went into the desert for 40 days and nights to be tempted.

He began preaching in Galilee and performing Miracles, but they don't count yet as beginning His ministry - as he wasn't preaching to the multitudes - the Gentiles yet.. An example would be the Marriage in Canaan when Jesus turns water into wine. He even said it wasn't time yet.

> **John 2:1-4** (NIV) [1]On the third day a wedding took place at Cana in Galilee. Jesus' mother was there, [2]and Jesus and his disciples had also been invited to the wedding. [3]When the wine was gone, Jesus' mother said to him, "They have no more wine."[4]"Woman, why do you involve me?" Jesus replied. "My hour has not yet come."

The Ministry of Jesus began during the **Sermon on the Mount** when the multitudes gathered and the foundation of Christianity was laid.

This happened after the best guessed time of His baptism by John on or around the celebrated Epiphany of January 6, making it closer to Spring in the year 29 AD.

My best guess would be around or after Passover in April 29 AD.

The Message was delivered with the Sermon on the Mount most likely in April 29 AD

Okay, so we've established Jesus' approximate birth in AD 4 and when He was filled with the Spirit and began His ministry in AD 29.

What about his crucifixion and resurrection?

Chapter 8

The Return

Establishing Jesus' Resurrection

Do we have an estimate on the date of the crucifixion of Jesus?

There are many ways to establish when Jesus was crucified. Some use non-Christian sources such as the writings of Josephus and Tacitus, in addition to working backwards from the historically well-established trial of Apostle Paul in Achaea to estimate the date of Paul's conversion. Using all these methods we get a range from the year 30 AD to 36 AD.

Most Historical and biblical scholars agree that Jesus was crucified between the years AD 30 and AD 36. Both methods of dating place the year 36 AD as an upper bound to Jesus' crucifixion.

This places our best estimates with Jesus as:

- born in 4 AD,
- beginning of His ministry in 29 AD, and
- His Crucifixion in 36 AD.

That puts a seven year gap between the start of His ministry and His crucifixion, which is strange because his ministry is believed to have only lasted 1 to 3 years. But, arguably, ALL of our records and estimates are sketchy at best.

We're going with:

- **Birth: 4 AD**
- **Ministry: 29 AD**
- **Crucifixion: 36 AD**

Why is His birth, ministry, and crucifixion so significant to all of this?

First of all, you may have noticed the dates don't quite mesh up with what's been preached and what the calendar hanging on your wall says.

First of, you must realize our calendar has changed a few times. Our current calendar is the Gregorian Calendar introduced in 1582, which replaced the Julian Calendar that took effect in 45 AD. Because of this and we humans learning more about astronomy and more accurate time keeping, dates have shifted a bit.

Because of these calendar changes, our recorded date of year 1 has changed. This is how Jesus could be born anywhere from 6 BC to 4 AD and not simply on year "1". The date was approximated when the calendar was created.

There are probably more things which we do not realize about Jesus besides his birth date, such as his name.

For starters, his name wasn't even "Jesus" until the few hundred years ago. "Jesus" is simply the mistranslated version we simply 'go with' these days.

It's not a big secret and it is common knowledge amongst clergy - it's really no big deal. We call him Jesus, so he's Jesus. He knows who we're talking about and quite frankly, none of us speak ancient Aramaic with accent and probably couldn't pronounce his name properly anyways.

I'll explain in the chapter 9 (next chapter), but you can skip past it to the chapter 10 if you're not interested.

Chapter 9

Lost in translation

Jesus' Name

What is Jesus' real name?

Jesus used in the English language originates from the Latin form of the Greek name Ἰησοῦς (Iēsous), a rendition of the Hebrew "Yeshua" (ישוע) or , also having the variants Joshua or Jeshua.

By the time the New Testament was written, the Septuagint (Greek biblical translation of the seventy interpreters, abbr as LXX) had already transliterated ישוי (Yeshua`) into "Koine Greek (also Alexandrian dialect, common Attic, Hellenistic or Biblical Greek, which was used from about 300 BC to around 300 AD (Byzantine official use until 1453 AD)) as closely as possible in the 3rd-century, the result being Ἰησοῦς (Iēsous).

75

Since Greek had no equivalent to the Semitic letter ש shin [ʃ], it was replaced with a σ sigma [s], and a masculine singular ending [-s] was added in the nominative case, in order to allow the name to be inflected for case (nominative, accusative, etc.) in the grammar of the Greek language. Basically, the ending s in Jesus was added when it was translated into Greek to indicate "Jesu" was male.

The diphthongal [a] vowel of Masoretic Yehoshua` or Yeshua` would not have been present in Hebrew/Aramaic pronunciation during this period, and some scholars believe some dialects dropped the pharyngeal sound of the final letter ע `ayin [ʕ], which in any case had no counterpart in ancient Greek.

The Greek writings of Philo of Alexandria and Josephus frequently mention this name. It also occurs in the Greek New Testament at Acts 7:45 and Hebrews 4:8, referring to Joshua son of Nun.

From Greek, Ἰησοῦς (Iēsous) moved into Latin at least by the time of the Vetus Latina. The morphological jump this time was not as large as previous changes between language families. Ἰησοῦς (Iēsous) was transliterated to Latin IESVS, where it stood for many centuries. The Latin name has an irregular declension, with a genitive, dative, ablative, and vocative of Jesu, accusative of Jesum, and nominative of Jesus. Minuscule (lower case) letters were developed around 800 AD and some time later the U was invented to distinguish the vowel sound from the consonantal sound and the J to distinguish the consonant from I. Similarly, Greek minuscules were invented about the same time, prior to that the name was written in Capital letters: ΙΗΣΟΥΣ, iota-eta-sigma, or ΙΗΣ sometime as: IHC or IHS with a line over the top I̅H̅C̅, I̅H̅Σ̅, I̅Σ̅ or I̅H̅S̅.

IHS monogram, with kneeling angels, atop the main altar, Church of the Gesù, Rome.

Most often simply expressed as ☧.

Modern English Jesus derives from Early Middle English Iesu (attested from the 12th century). The name participated in the Great Vowel Shift in late Middle English (15th century). The letter J was first distinguished from 'I' by the Frenchman Pierre

Ramus in the 16th century, but did not become common in Modern English until the 17th century, so that early 17th century works such as the first edition of the King James Version of the Bible (1611) continued to print the name with an I.

From the Latin, the English language takes the forms "Jesus" (from the nominative form), and "Jesu" (from the vocative and oblique forms). "Jesus" is the predominantly used form, while "Jesu" lingers in some more archaic texts.

In sum, this man claimed to be God and used the sacred name of God (YHWH) to call himself. This is why the Jews had him crucified for blasphemy, according tor Jewish law, they were suppose to stone him to death, but it was governed by Rome at the time and they handed such matters (i.e. the method of crucifixion).

I only explained the differences in calendars/dates and Jesus' name so hopefully now you understand the certain inaccuracies and why they exist on the current modern dates.

But again, I implore you to check the math and figures yourself.

Chapter 10

It all adds up

The Timeline

Okay, back to where we left off: we established Jesus' Birth, Ministry, and Crucifixion.

Let us now talk about the future and what's been predicted by the prophets and what was straight out foretold to us by Jesus himself.

Now realize, I am fully aware of Mark 13:32 where is makes very clear that we will not know the hour or the day. As well as Matthew 25:13.

> **Matthew 25:13** (ISV) So keep on watching, because you don't know the day or the hour.

And I understand it 's been made clear that it will be a sudden surprise, such as *a thief in the night*.

> **1 Thessalonians 5:2** (ISV) for you yourselves know very well that the Day of the Lord will come like a thief in the night.

We are told that we won't know when He comes and that it will be a sudden surprise, but we are also told that it be revealed and we will know when it is near.

> **Matthew 24:33** (ISV) In the same way, when you see all these things, you'll know that the Son of Man is near, right at the door.

When He comes, it will be a surprise to most, except to those paying attention and keeping aware – as He told us to do!

> **Revelation 16:15** (ISV) "See, I am coming like a thief. How blessed is the person who remains alert and keeps his clothes on! He won't have to go naked and let others see his shame."

To walk around 'naked' is to walk around in ignorance. We've been told over and over throughout the Bible when He's Coming. It's been revealed to us from the very beginning. Summed up in the Bible, we're taught a very brief history of Creation (Ἐν ἀρχῇ), a history of the First Chosen (the Jews), prophecies of a coming Savior (Messiah), the Savior's arrival (Jesus), notification of the Savior's Return, and the Coming of the Lord.

All things in the Bible are past tense, except for the Return of the Savior and Coming of the Lord's Kingdom. All writings and books speak of the Coming of the Lord's Kingdom on Earth.

From the Christian point of view, every Commandment, teaching, prophecy, and even our Redemption from the Original Sin, is all focused in anticipation of either going to Heaven after we die or for the Coming of the Lord and His Kingdom – *depending on one's personal beliefs*.

Most Christian beliefs hold that the writings of the prophets and what was directly foretold by Jesus himself, is that there will be a rapturing or collection of souls as He passes, then seven years of Tribulation, followed by His Second Coming. After these events take place, then the Lord comes personally to rule forever in His Kingdom.

We all know the story and have heard all this **End of the World** bible thumping our whole lives.

There's always someone coming out with a sign or prediction. I've lost count of how many times the world was suppose to come to an end in my lifetime alone.

There's no denial that events in everyone's lifetime through the Ages make it seem like the End of Times are coming. Especially during the last century of World Wars.

Nothing brings out the evil of humanity than a bitter global war and the signs in Revelations seem to be something happening all over the place, ALL the time.

So what makes me believe it's now time for the Rapture, Great Tribulation, and Second Coming?

The Timeline after Christ

Following this baseline set by Christ and all the Prophets, according to your bible and beliefs (*or not*).

We are taught that after Jesus was executed, Christ was resurrected and went to Heaven. From that point in time the Age of the Church, also known as the Age of the Gentile, began. This period of time lasts for 2000 years, after which Jesus comes by and gathers the saints in what's commonly called "the Rapture".

He notes that when He gathers the saints, that it is not His Return and that He is just passing by to collect them. After this event takes place, there will be seven years of the Anti-Christ and a Great Tribulation until the actual Return of Christ which begins the Millennium (1000 years) until the eternal New Kingdom of the Lord.

The Return after seven years of Tribulation is

what is commonly referred to as "the Second Coming of Christ".

Here are the events as we were told they are suppose to take place in order:

> Birth → Ministry → Resurrection → Church Age (Age of the Gentile) → Rapture → Tribulation → Millennium → Lord's Kingdom

I am sure you already know the story, so here's the timeline visualized below:

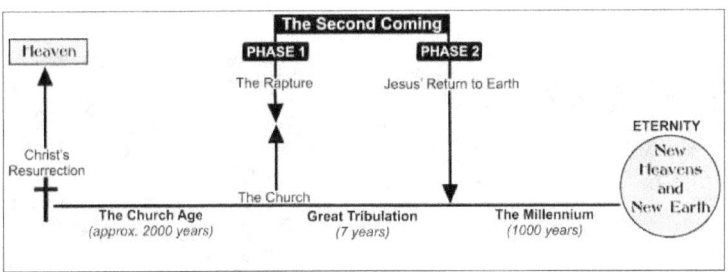

According to the timeline given to us *(explained in the following chapter)*, we are currently in the end of the Age of the Church (Age of the Gentile). This is the period of time which began with the Ministry of Jesus when He delivered His Word and it began to spread across the world.

We established the date of His Ministry to have happened most probably in the year 29 AD. This was when the Message was delivered with the Sermon on the Mount. We established that date from records and from Jewish holy dates which are set by cycles of the Moon.

The Message was delivered in April 29 AD.

April 13, 2029 marks the 2000th Anniversary of the beginning of Jesus' ministry.

On April 13, 2029, the near-Earth asteroid **Apophis 99942** will pass very close to Earth. It will roar thunderously across the sly from east to west, leaving behind it a stream that looks like parting skies.

It will be the 2000th anniversary of when "The Word" was delivered from the Sermon on the Mount which began the Age of the Gentile (the Age of the Church) will have come to an end with the rapture (gathering).

So where do we get this 2000 year timeline and what's the significant of events happening?

Chapter 11

A couple of days

Two Thousand Years

So where do we get this 2000 year timeline?

We get it from several sources in the Bible. One source is from the Book of Hosea from the Hebrew Bible (Old Testament) where we are told that after two days he will raise us.

> **Hosea 6:2** (KJV) After two days will he revive us: in the third day he will raise us up, and we shall live in his sight..

That is, after two days he will raise those up on the third day.

This was repeated in the Gospel of Matthew.

> **Matthew 17:23** (NIV) They will kill him, and on the third day he will be raised to life. And

the disciples were filled with grief.

We get 2000 years from this because it was also pointed out quite bluntly that one(1) human/earth day = 1000 years to The Lord.

> **2 Peter 3:8** (NIV)"But do not forget this one thing, dear friends: With the Lord a day is like a thousand years, and a thousand years are like a day."

A thousand years equaling one day to The Lord was also expressed in The Book of Psalms in the Old Testament.

> **Psalm 90:4** (NIV) A thousand years in your sight are like a day that has just gone by, or like a watch in the night.

From this it is understood that after two (2) days He will raise us up. With a day of the Lord equaling 1000 years to humans, then "two days" means "two-thousand years".

He will return to raise us in two-thousand years.

In the Book of Daniel, we are also given a time frame of when the Lord's people will be raptured:

> **Daniel 9:24-26** (NIV) Seventy weeks have been decreed concerning your people and your holy city: to restrain transgression, to put an end to sin, to make atonement for lawlessness, to establish everlasting righteousness, to

conclude vision and prophecy, and to anoint the Most Holy Place. ²⁵So be informed and discern that seven weeks and 62 weeks will elapse from the issuance of the command to restore and rebuild Jerusalem until the Anointed Commander. The plaza and moat will be rebuilt, though in troubled times. ²⁶Then after the 62 weeks, the anointed one will be cut down (but not for himself). Then the people of the Coming Commander will destroy both the city and the Sanctuary. Its ending will come like a flood, and until the end there will be war, with desolations having been decreed.

This prophecy by Daniel is commonly referred to as "The 70 Weeks of Years." This name derives from the opening words of most English translations: "Seventy weeks have been decreed". In the Hebrew, the word translated "weeks" is actually the word "sevens." So, the text actually says, "Seventy sevens have been decreed…"

The 70 Weeks of Years. The time frame used is seven years or weeks of years and it's broken up into seven sevens to when Jerusalem is rebuilt; then sixty two sevens to when Jesus is crucified. This leaves the final seven as being the period of tribulation.

From Daniel's prophecy, mankind seems to have been given 'seven days,' (or seven thousand years) from the time of Adam until the completion of human history on the Day of the Lord (Judgment Day). Using Daniel's timeline, the period from Adam to Abraham lasted about 2,000 years, from Abraham to Christ was about 2,000 years, and the Messianic Age when Christ rules on earth is a Sabbath "day" of 1,000 years.

This leaves no more than 2,000 years for the Church Age (Age of the Gentile) to be completed before the Second Coming. This reinforces the timeline period of 2,000 year "days" given by Hosea and John in their prophesies.

The Age of the Church is also mentioned in the Gospel of Luke when Jesus speaks of future events, including the destruction of Jerusalem in regards to His return when He mentions the fulfilling of the **times of the Gentiles:**

> **Luke 21:24** (NIV) They will fall by the sword and will be taken as prisoners to all the nations. Jerusalem will be trampled on by the Gentiles **until the times of the Gentiles are fulfilled.**

In the Letter to Romans, there is similar phrase which says,

> **Romans 11:25** (KJV) For I would not, brethren, that ye should be ignorant of this mystery, lest ye should be wise in your own conceits; that blindness in part is happened to

Israel, **until the fullness of the Gentiles be come in.**

Does the Bible tell us what the phrase "times of the Gentiles" means?

The Old Testament also references the time of the gentiles when the sixth-century BC prophet and author of the Book of Ezekiel writes:

> **Ezekiel 30:3** (ISV) For comes now the day—comes now the Day of the LORD, the day of clouds! **The time of the gentiles is fulfilled!**

The visions of Daniel deal with Gentile world and those in control relating to their role in God's future plans for the earth. Nebuchadnezzar's image of gold, silver, bronze, iron, and clay *(Daniel 2:31–45)* represent the successive Gentile kingdoms that will reign and control global power until the day Christ returns and establishes His Kingdom.

The Four Beasts *(Daniel 7:1–27)* that Daniel seen in his visions are four nations who will dominate for a time until the Day of the Lord.

Daniel's vision of the ram and the goat *(Daniel 8:1–26)* gives more detail about these dominating Gentile nations and their time of rule.

In these visions given to Daniel, the Gentiles have complete dominion over the world and the Jews.

They dominate the planet for a while until the Lord ultimately comes, subdues them, and then brings His eternal Kingdom.

Each vision of Daniel refers to The Lord's Kingdom dominating in the end. These periods of the Gentile rule are all the years from the time of the Babylonian Empire of Nebuchadnezzar in 588 BC until the Day of the Lord with Christ returning to establish His Kingdom.

We are now living in final years of the 'times of the Gentiles' just prior to the Day of the Lord.

There are similar references to the time of Gentile dominion ending with the return of Christ in the Book of Revelation. In John's vision, he foretells that Jerusalem will be under Gentile control even after the Lord's Temple has been restored.

> **Revelation 11:2** (NIV) But exclude the outer court; do not measure it, because it has been given to the Gentiles. They will trample on the holy city for 42 months.

This control by Gentile nations concludes when the Armies of the Beast are destroyed by the Lord in Revelation 19:17–19. This is the precursor just before the reign of Christ is put in place for 1000 years.

During His Ministry, in the Testimony of Luke, Jesus mentions a time in which Jerusalem is under the control of Gentile rulers.

> **Luke 21:24** (NIV) They will fall by the sword and will be taken as prisoners to all the nations. Jerusalem will be trampled on by the Gentiles until the times of the Gentiles are fulfilled.

In Paul's Letter to the Romans, we're given the reasoning behind the times of the Gentiles. This is the period of time (2000 years) in which the Gospel of Christ is spread to the ends of the entire world. A period of time when the Gospel is heard by every ear.

> **Romans 11:25** (NIV) I do not want you to be ignorant of this mystery, brothers and sisters, so that you may not be conceited: Israel has experienced a hardening in part until the full number of the Gentiles has come in

The message from Paul in Romans 11 is that, when the Jewish people rejected Christ, they were temporarily cut off from the blessings of a relationship with God. Because of this, Christ's gospel was delivered to the Gentiles, who gladly receive it.

When the time has come and the Word has been spread throughout the world, the Lord will restore the nation of Israel bringing an end to "the times of the Gentiles" (Isaiah 17:7; 62:11–12; Romans 11:26).

This Time of the Gentiles is the two-thousand year period prior to the coming of the Lord.

Chapter 12

Collecting the first fruits

The Rapture

What is the Rapture?

From the teachings of Jesus, of the Apostles, and of the prophecies told in both the Old and New Testaments, we are told that there will be an event which is part of the Second Coming of The Lord Jesus Christ. Many followers of Christ believe that His Second Coming will be in two phases, not just Him simply returning after a given time.

This first part of "The Second Coming" is said to happen after "two days" *(2000 years)* when Christ will pass-by to collect the souls of His believers, both dead and alive.

The second phase will occur just **BEFORE** He returns to Earth permanently to prepare the way for

The Lord's New Kingdom in what is commonly called, 'The Second Coming of Christ'.

It is believed from prophecy and from what the Apostles have directly testified, that 'when the time has come', Christ will pass by Earth to gather His believers who were saved by Him and have held fast to their faith, both living and dead.

This event is what is commonly referred to as the "gathering" or "rapturing" of believers, as told in Paul's First Epistle to the Thessalonians.

> **1 Thessalonians 4:13-17** (NIV) [13]Brothers and sisters, we do not want you to be uninformed about those who sleep in death, so that you do not grieve like the rest of mankind, who have no hope. [14]For we believe that Jesus died and rose again, and so we believe that God will bring with Jesus those who have fallen asleep in him. [15]According to the Lord's word, we tell you that we who are still alive, who are left until the coming of the Lord, will certainly not precede those who have fallen asleep. [16]For the Lord himself will come down from heaven, with a loud command, with the voice of the archangel and with the trumpet call of God, and the dead in Christ will rise first. [17]After that, we who are still alive and are left will be caught up together with them in the clouds to meet the Lord in the air. And so we will be with the Lord forever.

What the Apostle Paul is saying in this letter to the Thessalonians is when this event happens, as was foretold by Christ Himself, there will be a transformation and 'catching up' (rapturing) of all Christians, dead and alive, to meet with Him in the air as He passes by.

This will **NOT** be obvious to the world as many nonbelievers like to ridicule. You won't see Christ in the skies all obvious to the world, and you will not see people suddenly lifting up and floating off into the sky. It will be secret and unknown to the world of unbelievers at the time of its happening.

A closer examination at 1 Corinthians 15:52 helps clarify this.

> **1 Corinthians 15:52** (NIV) in a flash, in the twinkling of an eye, at the last trumpet. For the trumpet will sound, the dead will be **raised imperishable**, and **we will be changed**.

In the verse, "imperishable" is also commonly translated as "incorruptible", such as is written in the King James Version:

> **1 Corinthians 15:52** (KJV) In a moment, in the twinkling of an eye, at the last trumpet: for the trumpet shall sound, and the dead shall be raised **incorruptible**, and we shall be changed.

Here is the original Greek (modern) taken from the original Koine Greek *(Biblical Greek)*, which was used in Paul's Epistle to the Corinthians:

ΠΡΟΣ ΚΟΡΙΝΘΙΟΥΣ Α΄ 15:52 (SBLGNT)
ἐν ἀτόμῳ, ἐν ῥιπῇ ὀφθαλμοῦ, ἐν τῇ ἐσχάτῃ σάλπιγγι· σαλπίσει γάρ, καὶ οἱ νεκροὶ ἐγερθήσονται **ἄφθαρτοι**, καὶ ἡμεῖς ἀλλαγησόμεθα.

Translating the word ἄφθαρτοι in 1 Corinthians 15:52, we find that it is related to the word ἀφθαρσία which means incorruptibility, unending existence, immortality, incorruption, genuineness, sincerity, integrity. It is also related to the word ἄφθαρτος, which means: undecaying, incorruptible, immortal.

It is my assumption from these tranlsations that being **raised up** and **changed** in "imperishable", "incorruptible", or "immortal" bodies (or forms) means "Spirit".

This is what is meant by saying that the gathering (or rapturing) won't be noticeable to nonbelievers because they won't see people floating up in the sky towards The Lord. They won't even see The Lord.

Personally, I believe that those 'gathered' whom are still alive will appear to periodically die off by a variety of reasons, apparently natural and otherwise.

This is a gathering of those who had undying

faith. The unfaithful and nonbelievers will only see an asteroid blasting across the sky – and nothing more.

> **Revelation 14:4-5** (ISV) ⁴They have not defiled themselves with women, for they are virgins, and they follow the lamb wherever he goes. They have been redeemed from among humanity as the first fruits for God and the lamb. ⁵In their mouth no lie was found. They are blameless.

If there is to be a "rapturing' or 'gathering' of 'the Faithful', then why haven't the ancient prophets of the Bible mention it?

They did, as it is also prophesied in the Hebrew Bible (Old Testament) by Daniel.

> **Daniel 7:13** (NIV) In my vision at night I looked, and there before me was one like a **son of man, coming with the clouds of heaven**. He approached the Ancient of Days and was led into his presence.

So whats me believe that "the Rapture" is happening when asteroid Apophis 99942 passes earth April 2029?

Besides the fact that the asteroid passes exactly on the 2000ᵗʰ anniversary DAY of when His Ministry began?

This will happen after the foretold two days (two-thousand years) when the Lord reaps the fruits of what He has sown. On the 2000th anniversary of when He planted to seeds of His Word.

The asteroid Apophis 999942 will pass us exactly as He said it would, splitting the skies.

On April 13, 2029, the near-Earth asteroid **Apophis 99942** will pass very close to Earth and roar thunderously across the sky from east to west. It will be a grand show and you can guarantee that it will get more media coverage than did *the solar eclipse*.

When it passes, it will leave behind a cloud stream along its path which will look very much like skies are parting.

It will look very much like what you often see depicted in many 'end of the world" science fiction films. Most people won't think of it much more than any other near-Earth celestial object.

When Apophis 99942 passes by, it will look much like the 25-foot asteroid that passed over California in the year 2004 – except much bigger.

The asteroid that passed over California came within 186,000 miles of Earth's surface in the picture captured *(next page)* on May 5th, 2004.

PASADENA, Calif., May 5, 2014 (UPI) -- A 25-foot asteroid passed between Earth and the moon, coming within 186,000 miles of Earth's surface. On average, the moon's orbit is 238,855 miles from Earth.

On April 13th 2029, Asteroid Apophis 99942 will pass dangerously close leaving a cloud trail behind it in a similar manner as the much smaller asteroid that passed over California in 2014.

News of this coming asteroid WAS in the international news in 2004. Unfortunately at the same time it was announced to the world, the devastating 2004 Indian Ocean Tsunami happened and dominated the news.

Nobody paid any attention to the giant rock coming at us.

When it passes, it flash across the sky very quickly and pass at an angle which most probably will appear as if it is going from east to west.

When asteroid Apophis 999942 streams across the sky in April 2029, it will look exactly as had been described by Jesus to His Disciples.

> **Matthew 24:27** (NIV) For as lightning that comes from the east is visible even in the west, so will be the coming of the Son of Man.

> **Luke 17:24** (NIV) For as the lightning flashes and lights up the sky from one end to the other, so will be the Son of Man in His day.

Because it will be passing quickly and very close, close enough leave burning clouds across the sky, it will also **roar across the sky** very 'thunderously' much like other objects have in the past.

> **Matthew 24:30** (NIV) Then will appear the sign of the Son of Man in heaven. And then all the peoples of the earth will mourn when they see the Son of Man coming on the clouds of heaven, with power and great glory. [31]And he will send his angels with a loud trumpet call, and they will gather his elect from the four winds, from one end of the heavens to the other.

This is also mentioned in the Book of Revelations.

> **Revelations 1:7** (NIV) "Look, he is coming with the clouds," and "every eye will see him, even those who pierced him"; and all peoples on earth "will mourn because of him." So shall it be! Amen.

This 'rapturing' has been mentioned many times.

> **John 14:3-4** (NIV) ³And if I go and prepare a place for you, I will come back and take you to be with me that you also may be where I am. ⁴You know the way to the place where I am going.

The asteroid (Christ and those He carried away *(Raptured)*) with Him will then pass by and not return for a period of seven years.

In the New Testament, it says He only gathers *(raptures)* as He passes *(this is NOT the Second Coming)* and then He won't return for a period of seven years, which is called the Great Tribulation.

The Great Tribulation will last for seven (7) years and then Christ will return. The return is the Second Coming of Christ.

Who will be left behind at the rapture – the foolish virgins

When Christ spoke of the wise and foolish virgins in Matthew 25 verses 1-13, He explains to us clearly that not all believers will be gathered up in the 'rapture'.

These are the "foolish virgins" which will be the ones who will be left behind with the unbelievers.

Matthew 25:1-13 (ISV) ¹"At that time, the kingdom from heaven will be comparable to ten bridesmaids who took their oil lamps and went out to meet the groom. ²Now five of them were foolish, and five were wise, ³because when the foolish ones took their lamps, they didn't take any oil with them. ⁴But the wise ones took flasks of oil with their lamps. ⁵Since the groom was late, all of them became sleepy and lay down. ⁶But at midnight there came a shout: 'The groom is here! Come out to meet him!' ⁷Then all the bridesmaids woke up and got their lamps ready. ⁸"But the foolish ones told the wise, 'Give us some of your oil, because our lamps are going out!' ⁹"But the wise ones replied, 'No! There will never be enough for us and for you. You'd better go to the dealers and buy some for yourselves.' ¹⁰"While they were away buying it, the groom arrived. Those who were ready went with him into the wedding banquet, and the door was closed. ¹¹Later, the other bridesmaids arrived and said, 'Lord, lord, open up for us!' ¹²"But he replied, 'I tell all of you with certainty, I don't know you!' ¹³So keep on watching, because you don't know the day or the hour."

These are the ones that do not have a hidden life with Christ in God, but lived by His teachings and remained pure in His eyes. They are the ones who will not deny fellowship in Christ during persecution.

> **Matthew 13:21** (NIV) ²¹But since they have no root, they last only a short time. When trouble or persecution comes because of the word, they quickly fall away.

Although they have a good outward appearance and appear to be righteous, they are still living a hidden life in sin. In sum, even though they know they are in the wrong, they continue doing what they know to be wrong.

> **Revelation 3:1-3** (ISV) ¹"To the messenger of the church in Sardis, write: 'The one who has the seven spirits of God and the seven stars says this: 'I know what you've been doing. You are known for being alive, but you are dead. ²Be alert, and strengthen the things that are left, which are about to die. I note that your actions are incomplete before my God. ³So remember what you received and heard. Obey it, and repent. If you are not alert, I will come like a thief, and you won't know the time when I will come to you.

But for those who are walking in the light as He instructed them, those He will gather as the 'first fruits'.

> **1 John 1:7** (ISV) ⁷But if we keep living in the light as he himself is in the light, we have fellowship with one another, and the blood of Jesus his Son cleanses us from all sin.

There is absolutely no reason to be anxious about the Lord's gathering of the 'first fruits' (the Rapture). It is a time to look forward to. A day to await with joyful expectation. It is the end goal of every follower of Christ. To follow His teachings and be ready for the day when He comes for them.

To be gathered by the Lord and be given the Gift of Eternal Life.

Will I be along in the rapture?

> **Luke 9:23** (ISV) [23]Then he told all of them, "If anyone wants to come with me, he must deny himself, pick up his cross every day, and follow me continuously,

Are you giving up your own will and fleshly, worldly desires and out your faith in Christ? By denying yourself in order to be a disciple of Christ?

> **1 John 3:3** (NIV) All who have this hope in him purify themselves, just as he is pure.

Those will be the 'first fruits' of which He gathers when He passes in 2029.

Chapter 13

Time to awaken

Seven years of Tribulation

The Tribulation is a relatively short period of time which will last for seven years. The Tribulation is referenced throughout the Bible and is often referred to by other names, such as: being a time of distress, suffering, anguish, trouble, or oppression (Deuteronomy 4:30, Zephaniah 1:1, Matthew 24:21, Daniel 12:1, Zephaniah 1:15).

In the books of Isaiah 2:12; 13:6-9, Joel 1:15; 2:1-31; 3:14, and 1 Thessalonians 5:2, it's referred to as being the Day of the Lord. The book of Jeremiah 30:7 calls it a time of Jacob's trouble.

The seven years of the Great Tribulation will be broken up into two halves. Occurrences in the first half of 3 ½ years will seem no different than they are today. There are a few specific signs mentioned, but for the most part it will go predominately unnoticed to the world as had the Rapturing event. However, the second 3 ½ years will not go unnoticed. It will be a time when worldwide catastrophes will affect and be experienced by everyone on the planet. It will be a period of time in which the world will be in a state of great trouble.

A time of great suffering will be placed upon mankind. A time of great suffering which has not occurred from the beginning of the creation and will not occur again.

> **Mark 13:19** (NIV) because those will be days of distress unequaled from the beginning, when God created the world, until now—and never to be equaled again.

The tribulation is a period not only predicted in the New Testament by Christ, but also by the prophets in the Old Testament.

> **Daniel 12:1** (NIV) "At that time Michael, the great prince who protects your people, will arise. There will be a time of distress such as has not happened from the beginning of nations until then. But at that time your people —everyone whose name is found written in the book—will be delivered.

Daniel also defined the length of the Tribulation

in his prophesies. He said God would accomplish all His purposes for the Jewish people during a period of 70 weeks of years *(totaling 490 years (70 weeks = 70 x 7))*. Sixty-nine of those weeks of years *(483 years)* would lead up to the death of the Messiah. The final week of years would occur at the end of the age, right before the return of the Messiah *(Daniel 9:24-27)*.

> **Daniel 9:24-27** (NIV) [24]"Seventy 'sevens' are decreed for your people and your holy city to finish transgression, to put an end to sin, to atone for wickedness, to bring in everlasting righteousness, to seal up vision and prophecy and to anoint the Most Holy Place. [25]"Know and understand this: From the time the word goes out to restore and rebuild Jerusalem until the Anointed One, the ruler, comes, there will be seven 'sevens,' and sixty-two 'sevens.' It will be rebuilt with streets and a trench, but in times of trouble. [26]After the sixty-two 'sevens,' the Anointed One will be put to death and will have nothing. The people of the ruler who will come will destroy the city and the sanctuary. The end will come like a flood: War will continue until the end, and desolations have been decreed. [27]He will confirm a covenant with many for one 'seven.' In the middle of the 'seven' he will put an end to sacrifice and offering. And at the temple he will set up an abomination that causes desolation, until the end that is decreed is poured out on him.

This concluding week of years (7 years) corresponds to the Tribulation for, as Daniel put it, it will mark the time when "the prince who is to come" will "make desolate" — a reference to the Antichrist. This is who Jesus called the "abomination that causes desolation" in Matthew 24:15.

> **Matthew 24:15** (NIV) "So when you see standing in the holy place 'the abomination that causes desolation,' spoken of through the prophet Daniel—let the reader understand—

This is "the beast" who is referred to in Revelation 13.

Daniel continues to explain that the beast will make a covenant for seven years, but in the middle of this week (3 1/2 years into the tribulation) he will then break the covenant.

> **Daniel 9:27** (NIV) He will confirm a covenant with many for one 'seven.' In the middle of the 'seven' he will put an end to sacrifice and offering. And at the temple he will set up an abomination that causes desolation, until the end that is decreed is poured out on him.

Referencing the beast, the book of Revelations tells of the Tribulation's mid-points lasting 1260 days and 42 months

> **Revelation 11:2-3** (NIV) [2]But exclude the outer court; do not measure it, because it has been given to the Gentiles. They will trample

on the holy city for 42 months. ³And I will appoint my two witnesses, and they will prophesy for 1,260 days, clothed in sackcloth."

Revelation 13 explains that the beast will place an image of himself in the temple and require the world to worship him. Revelation 13:5 says that this will go on for 42 months, which is 3 1/2 years. Since Daniel 9:27 says that this will happen in the middle of the week and Revelation 13:5 says that the beast will do this for a period of 42 months, it is easy to see that the total length of time is 84 months or seven years. This time frame is also given in Daniel 7:25, where the "time, times, and half a time" (time=1 year; times=2 years; half a time=1/2 year; total of 3 1/2 years) also refers to period of the 'great tribulation'. Also noted is that the last half of the seven-year tribulation period when the beast will be in power.

During this time mankind will experience global disasters such as famine, war, pain, and suffering for seven years before the Second Coming of Christ takes place. Most believe the worse will occur during the final half of the Tribulation, during the last 3 ½ years.

> **2 Timothy 3:1** (NIV) But mark this: There will be terrible times in the last days.
>
> **Romans 2:9** (NIV) There will be trouble and

distress for every human being who does evil: first for the Jew, then for the Gentile;

This time of great suffering will be experienced by those who weren't collected *(raptured)* by Christ before the period of great tribulations and were lucky to be spared.

The Great Tribulation are the final seven years before Armageddon

Jesus foretold about a time of great tribulation that will be experienced in the Olivet Discourse (also known as the 'Prophecy on the Mount of Olives' or 'Olivet Prophecy'). He used the description similar to that used by the prophet Daniel in His discourse.

> **Matthew 24:21-22** (NIV) [21]For then there will be great distress, unequaled from the beginning of the world until now—and never to be equaled again. [22]"If those days had not been cut short, no one would survive, but for the sake of the elect those days will be shortened.

The Olivet Prophesy is in the New Testament books of Matthew 24, Mark 13, and Luke 21.

We are told from Luke's Gospel that Jesus taught over a period of time at the Jerusalem Temple and then stayed on the Mount of Olives at night, which was just opposite the Temple.

It was during this time that the 'Olivet Discourse' was given.

In the Gospels of Matthew and Mark, Jesus spoke this prophecy to his disciples privately on the Mount of Olives. This was when Jesus' warned about the suffering during a period of tribulation and of persecution that will be experienced.

The discourse begins when a disciple remarked on the greatness of Herod's Temple (the 2nd Temple) and Jesus responded saying that not one of those stones would remain intact in the building and that the entire temple building would be reduced to rubble.

> **Matthew 24:1-2** (NIV) [1]Jesus left the temple and was walking away when his disciples came up to him to call his attention to its buildings. [2]"Do you see all these things?" he asked. "Truly I tell you, not one stone here will be left on another; every one will be thrown down."

The disciples, being Jewish, believed that the Messiah would come and that his arrival would mean the fulfillment of all the prophecies they hoped in. They believed that the Temple played a large role in this, hence the disciple in the first part boasting to Jesus about the Temple's construction.

Jesus' prophecy on the Mount of Olives

concerning the Temple's destruction was contrary to their belief system.

Jesus sought to correct that impression, first, by discussing the Roman invasion in the Book of **Matthew 24:4–34**, and then by commenting on his final coming to render universal judgment in **Matthew 24:35–51**.

Christ pointed out both the signs of which will hail His coming AND that His coming will be a sudden surprise, like a thief in the night with the hour and day not known by the unbelieving.

The Book of Revelation (6:1-17; 8:1-6) marks the first stages of the Great Tribulation by the breaking of Seven Seals in Heaven and it culminates in the rapture of the bride of Christ up to heaven and the harlot being cast off of the beast's back. The breaking of the Seventh Seal introduces the Seven Trumpet Judgments, ending the first quarter of the Tribulation period and preparing for an even worse period called the "Day of Wrath."

The second stage in Revelation is marked by the blowing of seven trumpets in heaven. This is a period where the beast will be in contention with the "Second Fruits". The Second Fruits those who strayed and were not collected in the Rapture but choose now to serve the Lord.

As mentioned in the previous chapter, if you believe in Christ but were not Raptured - do not be worried. There can be a number of reasons why of which we do not know and it does not mean He is not coming for you. Perhaps you are not ready or possibly it's felt that you should remain to help guide others. Those are answers we won't have until it's all over and done.

If you were not Raptured, but stay true during the time of trials, He WILL come back for you.

> **Deuteronomy 4:30** (NIV) When you are in distress and all these things have happened to you, then in later days you will return to the Lord your God and obey him.

This stage ends in the reaping of the "second fruits" up to heaven and Satan being thrown out of heaven and down to earth.

> **Revelation 2:10** (NIV) Do not be afraid of what you are about to suffer. I tell you, the devil will put some of you in prison to test you, and you will suffer persecution for ten days. Be faithful, even to the point of death, and I will give you life as your victor's crown.

According to the Bible, this seven-year period called the Tribulation will be divided into two halves. In the first half, the Antichrist appears to be the great benefactor and protector and friend of

Israel. However in the middle of that period lasting 7 years, he will turn against the people of Israel and begin desolating it severely.

Many Christians believe the second half will be the worse of the period of Trials. A time of which has never occurred since the beginning of the world or ever will happen again.

The second half of this 70th week of Daniel 9 will be the unparalleled time of trouble for the world

When the final seven years begins, the Book of Revelation states that the Temple Mount in Jerusalem will be placed under a sharing arrangement between Jews and Muslims and the Jewish people will be allowed to build their Third Temple on the Temple Mount.

> **Revelation 11:1-2** (NIV) [1]Then there was given me a measuring rod like a staff; and someone said, "Get up and measure the temple of God and the altar, and those who worship in it. [2]"Leave out the court which is outside the temple and do not measure it, for it has been given to the nations; and they will tread under foot the holy city for forty-two months.
>
> **2 Thessalonians 2:4** (NIV) He will oppose and will exalt himself over everything that is called God or is worshiped, so that he sets himself up in God's temple, proclaiming himself to be God.

When the temple is completed, animal sacrifices will be resumed (Daniel 9:27), just as was done in Old Testament times.

> **Daniel 9:27** (NIV) He will confirm a covenant with many for one 'seven.' In the middle of the 'seven' he will put an end to sacrifice and offering. And at the temple he will set up an abomination that causes desolation, until the end that is decreed is poured out on him."

This will quickly lead to an event the Bible calls the 'Abomination of Desolation' Jesus warned His disciples about.

All of this takes place in the period that will immediately precede the Battle of Armageddon and the Second Coming of Jesus to the earth.

Persecution against followers of Christ will be heavily persecuted during this period of time.

> **Matthew 24:9** (NIV) Then you will be handed over to be persecuted and put to death, and you will be hated by all nations because of me.

But fear not, it does not mean you are condemned. It simply means He will gather you among the 'second fruits' when He returns.

Chapter 14

The second fruits

The Second Coming

On Easter Sunday, April 13, 2036, exactly 2000 years to the day of when Jesus rose from the dead, asteroid Apophis 99942 will impact Earth.

Scientists have calculated that the asteroid will 'passover' us on April 13, 2029 with a great show. As the first passover flew over reaping the first born, the Lord will passover and reap (rapture) the first fruits.

Seven years of terrible times which have never been experienced before will then plague the earth.

Then comes the terrible Day of the Lord.

The Day of the Apocalypse.

The asteroid will impact Earth on Easter Sunday April 13, 2036. Whether the asteroid is Christ's chariot or Wormwood falling to the earth after the third angel blows their trumpet (Rev 8:10–11), I don't know. I just know NASA confirmed the asteroid is coming, its passing, and impact date which match precisely with Biblical prophecy. This includes the damage and aftermath.

They estimate the force of Apophis 99942's impact to make atmospheric entry with 750 megatons of kinetic energy, instantly killing more than 10 million people.

> **Isaiah 24:6** (NIV) So a curse will destroy the earth. The people of the world are guilty, so they will be burned up; only a few will be left.

Exactly 2000 years to the day of when He rose from the dead. The flesh body of Jesus was crucified, then after two days he rose from the dead on the third day.

> **2 Peter 3:8** (NIV) But do not forget this one thing, dear friends: With the Lord a day is like a thousand years, and a thousand years are like a day.

Two-thousand years (two days to the Lord) have passed since the Lord came to us in the flesh. This is the foretold (and demonstrated) return of Christ after two days *(to the Lord, 2000 years to us)*. The weeks of Daniel have come a conclusion. It is the time they told us would come. Bad news to some, good news to others.

> **Matthew 24:30** (NIV) Then will appear the sign of the Son of Man in heaven. And then all the peoples of the earth will mourn when they see the Son of Man coming on the clouds of heaven, with power and great glory.

The Second Coming is the literal return of Christ to earth fulfilling His promise and prophecy to reign for a thousand years (Revelation 20:1-6).

The approach, passing, and arrival of this asteroid all coincide with prophecies.

> **Revelation 19:11-12** (NIV) [11]I saw heaven standing open and there before me was a white horse, whose rider is called Faithful and True. With justice he judges and wages war. [12]His eyes are like blazing fire, and on his head are many crowns. He has a name written on him that no one knows but he himself.

This is when the Lord punishes the wicked and rewards to faithful. The time all believers await. The time when evil is purged and a time of peace is brought.

It is the prophesied great and terrible day of the Lord. But only the wicked need worry – the faithful have long awaited the coming of this day.

Chapter 15

You decide

Conclusion

So, there's a giant rock hurling towards us.

Wow, that's a lot to take in.

So what's happening is: **Jesus is on His way.**

I don't know, take it for what it is. This is what I chanced across out of the blue and I felt that it was important enough to share with the world.

Either way, hey, there's a giant rock hurling towards us and it's going to cause an apocalypse.

It'll pass us on April 13, 2029 with a great show and then seven years later it will impact Earth on Easter Sunday April 13, 2036.

They're working on it, but don't hold your breath.

Personally, the timeline and dates are way too related to biblical prophecies for me to ignore. I think it's unfolding just as Christ explained it would to us. He told us He's coming and it looks like He is. I'm not going to preach the Gospel (any more than I already have), because there's no need for me to. The Word has been spread to the far ends of the planet in every language,

Everyone knows and has been told about the Gospel (another sign He's coming).

He flat out told us when and what the signs would be. The signs have come. The prophecies say it's time. Christ flat out told us it would be this time.

I am not a prophet and I am not predicting anything. I am only pointing out the prophecies, what scientists say is coming, and the fact the math seems to add up. I am merely reporting what I came across and letting you decide. Personally, I am convinced.

I realize the Bible states that we will not know the hour or the day, but here's where the Bible contradicts itself because we were also given signs to watch for and even a two-thousand year countdown of when He told us He was coming. He (and several prophets) even told us what what going to happen, how, and why – the very reason we KNOW He's coming.

So which is it? Either we won't know when He's coming or we know when He's coming because He told us when. I think the thief in the night and not knowing the hour or day was a warning for unbelievers. They will be the ones who will ignore the signs given to the believers who will see it clearly.

We also have to remember our sources as well. The bible and scriptures of which we are given are limited at best and confusing most of the time, especially where it contradicts itself in many instances. This is because we tend to forget the Bible we read was translated, written, and printed by fallible humans.

For example, the Council of Laodicea was formed in 363 AD after the war between the Roman Empire and the Persian Empire, which was waged by Emperor Julian.

Julian wanted to revive paganism and persecute the Christians, but he died on the battlefield and his generals hastily appointed Jovian as the new Emperor of Rome.

Jovian was a Christian and was the one who made many of the initial decisions about the Christian faith. He did this by forming the Council of Laodicea in 363-364 AD. This council of about thirty select clergy created Christianity's Canon by deciding on church rules and religious conduct. They also decided which books would be added to the bible and how they would be translated. They also decided what Apostolic writings would NOT be included and had them destroyed as heresy. Those who possessed knowledge of the other letters (not included as biblical canon) and testimonies were killed as heretics and their books and scrolls burned.

Other beliefs and writings were destroyed everywhere. Emperor Jovian called for the burning of the Library of Antioch which held nearly as much of a collection of knowledge as did the famous Library of Alexandria. It was marked as being pagan (and heretic) and burned down with all of its books and scrolls within it.

Even though the emperor died and was succeeded, the formed select church fathers continued to suppress and control the writing of the Apostles to suit their own desires.

Caesar is traditionally blamed for burning down the Library of Alexandria, but many testimonies say no. Part of it was reported as having burned, but most of the Library was saved and preserved. Many of the collections were moved to a "daughter library" in a temple known as the Serapeum of Alexandria.

Many original early Christian writings and testimonies of the Apostles and their disciples were housed there until the Church fathers from Rome were able to seize complete control of the region and called for the Library of the Serapeum of Alexandria (Library of Alexandria's surviving collection) to be burned in 391 AD for Heresy and Paganism.

Basically everything we know about God and Scriptures was decided for us in the 4th Century by a handful of power hungry guys in the Council of Laodicea (363-363 AD). They went out of their way to kill all others with full knowledge of God's word and burned all other writings.

How does God feel about this?

> **Revelation 3:14-16** (NIV) [14]"To the angel of the church in Laodicea write: These are the words of the Amen, the faithful and true witness, the ruler of God's creation. [15]I know your deeds, that you are neither cold nor hot. I wish you were either one or the other! [16]So, because you are lukewarm—neither hot nor cold—I am about to spit you out of my mouth.

He says they (the church fathers) are neither cold (totally wrong) or hot (totally right). They are "lukewarm" so he is going to spit them out (Judge and cast away).

In other words, God rejects the Church of Laodicea's decisions of what the Word of God is and what Scriptures to include and omit from the Bible.

Lukewarm because they contain lies (cold) mixed with the truth (hot).

This is our Bible, the words and beliefs which were decided for us in the 4th century by a handful of guys. Even with several reforms and the many branches of Protestantism, not much has changed at all from these initial decisions.

We didn't know any better either until later discoveries of lost scrolls and other books began to surface, such as the Dead Sea Scrolls, Nag Hammadi library, Sophia of Jesus Christ, Gospel of Thomas, etc..

We've missing much of the truth. So much that the Lord even proclaimed that during the Tribulation that He will send out an angel to spread the truth.

> **Revelation 14:6-7** (NIV) ⁶Then I saw another angel flying in midair, and he had the eternal gospel to proclaim to those who live on the earth—to every nation, tribe, language and people. ⁷He said in a loud voice, "Fear God and give him glory, because the hour of his judgment has come. Worship him who made the heavens, the earth, the sea and the springs of water."

Joyfully, we are soon going to learn the truth and peace is going to be brought to us.

But hey, you know what? I could be wrong or crazy. Take it for what it is.

Either way, there's an asteroid headed for us and it's going to cause an apocalypse – prophecy or not, it's still coming."

Check for yourself!

Sources

Richard Stone. "Target Earth". National Geographic Magazine, August 2008.

Nick J. Baileya, et al (2006). "Near Earth Object impact simulation tool for supporting the NEO mitigation decision making process". Cambridge University.

Binzel, Richard P. (2007). "Can NEAs be Grouped by Their Common Physical Characteristics?". Department of Earth, Atmospheric, and Planetary Sciences, Massachusetts Institute of Technology.

99942 Apophis (2004 MN4) "Earth Impact Risk Summary". Sentry: Earth Impact Monitoring. Center for Near-Earth Objects Studies, Jet Propulsion Laboratory, California Institute of Technology, NASA.

JPL Small-Body Database Browser: 99942 Apophis (2004 MN4)"

The Near-Earth Asteroids Data Base at E.A.R.N.

Pravec, P.; Scheirich, P.; Ďurech, J.; Pollock, J.; Kušnirák, P.; Hornoch, K.; Galád, A.; Vokrouhlický, D.; Harris, A.W.; Jehin, E.; Manfroid, J.; Opitom, C.; Gillon, M.; Colas, F.; Oey, J.; Vraštil, J.; Reichart, D.; Ivarsen, K.; Haislip, J.; LaCluyze, A. (2014). "The tumbling spin state of (99942) Apophis"

"Herschel intercepts asteroid Apophis". European Space Agency (ESA). 9 January 2013.

David Noland. "5 Plans to Head Off the Apophis Killer Asteroid". Popular Mechanics, November 7, 2006.

Don Yeomans; Steve Chesley & Paul Chodas. "Near-Earth Asteroid 2004 MN4 Reaches Highest Score To Date On Hazard Scale". NASA's Near Earth Object Program Office. December 23, 2004.

"MPEC 2004-Y70 : 2004 MN4". The International Astronomical Union (IAU) Minor Planet Center.

Don Yeomans; Paul Chodas & Steve Chesley. "Possibility of an Earth Impact in 2029 Ruled Out for Asteroid 2004 MN4". NASA's Near Earth Object Program Office, December 27, 2004.

Paul Chodas; Steve Chesley; Jon Giorgini & Don Yeomans. "Radar Observations Refine the Future Motion of Asteroid 2004 MN4". NASA's Near Earth Object Program Office, February 3, 2005.

Bill Cooke. "Asteroid Apophis set for a makeover". Astronomy Magazine, August 18, 2005.

Dwayne Brown. "NASA Refines Asteroid Apophis' Path Toward Earth". NASA's Near Earth Object Program Office, Oct 7, 2009.

Kelly Beatty. "Asteroid Apophis Takes a Pass in 2036". Sky & Telescope, January 9, 2013.

David Morrison. "Schweickart Proposes Study of Impact Risk from Apophis (MN4)". NASA, July 22, 2005.

University of Hawaii at Manoa's Institute for Astronomy, Honolulu. "Hawaii astronomers keep tabs on asteroid Apophis". Astronomy Magazine, March 10, 2011.

David Morrison (April 6, 2011). "Friday the 13th, 2029: Asteroid 2004 MN4 will come scarily close to Earth on April 13, 2029, but it will not hit.". science.nasa.gov.

"(99942) Apophis (Close Approaches)". NEODyS (Near Earth Objects—Dynamic Site).

"99942 Apophis Ephemerides for 9 Jan 2013". NEODyS (Near Earth Objects – Dynamic Site)

"(99942) Apophis Ephemerides for 13 Apr 2029". NEODyS (Near Earth Objects – Dynamic Site)

Dan Vergano. "Apophis asteroid encounter in 2013 should help answer impact worries". USA Today ScienceFair, 2010-11-10.

Dr. Lance A. M. Benner. "99942 Apophis 2013 Goldstone Radar Observations Planning". NASA/JPL Asteroid Radar Research, 2013-01-09.

Steve Chesley and Davide Farnocchia. "Apophis Risk Assessment Updated". Center for NEO Studies, Feb 21, 2013.

Brown, Dwayne. "NASA Refines Asteroid Apophis' Path Toward Earth". Jet Propulsion Laboratory, Pasadena, Calif. 2009-10-07.

Farnocchia, D.; Chesley, S. R.; Chodas, P. W.; Micheli, M.; Tholen, D. J.; Milani, A.; Elliott, G. T.; Bernardi, F.. "Yarkovsky-driven impact risk analysis for asteroid (99942) Apophis". Icarus, Volume 224, Issue 1, p. 192-200. (2013).

Range of Possible Impact Points on April 13, 2036 in Scenarios for Dealing with Apophis, by Donald B. Gennery, presented at the Planetary Defense Conference. Washington, DC. March 5–8, 2007.

Nick J. Baileya. "Near Earth Object impact simulation tool for supporting the NEO mitigation decision making process". Cambridge University Press, 2006.

Yu Fei. "Riding an asteroid: China's next space goal". Xinhua News, 7 March 2017.

Isachenkov, Vladimir. "Russia may send spacecraft to knock away asteroid". 2009-12-30.

"China Reveals Solar Sail Plan To Prevent Apophis Hitting Earth in 2036". Technology Review Physics. 2011-08-18.

"Russia wants to target near-Earth objects with its ICBMs". TASS 2016-02-15.

Gilmore, et al. Monthly Weather Review, Vol.132. American Meteorological Society, November 2004.

Alexander Roberts (Ed), James Donaldson (Ed), Philip Schaff (Ed), Henry Wace (Ed). Nicene and Post-Nicene Fathers, Second Series, Vol. 14. Hendrickson Pub, 1996. ISBN 978-1565631168.

Jerry Vardaman and Edwin M. Yamauchi. Chronos, Kairos, Christos: Nativity and Chronological Studies Presented to Jack Finegan. Eisenbrauns, 1989. ISBN 978-0931464508

Paul Barnett. Jesus & the Rise of Early Christianity: A History of New Testament Times. IVP Academic, 2002. ISBN 978-0830826995

Andreas J. Köstenberger and L. Scott Kellum. The Cradle, the Cross, and the Crown: An Introduction to the New

Testament. B&H Academic, 2009. ISBN 978-0805443653

E. P. Sanders. The Historical Figure of Jesus. Penguin Books, 1996. ISBN 978-0140144994

www.ingramcontent.com/pod-product-compliance
Lightning Source LLC
Chambersburg PA
CBHW071630080526
44588CB00010B/1347